W9-AQR-234

Village on the Seine

Bonnières at the turn of the twentieth century

Village on the Seine

TRADITION AND CHANGE IN BONNIÈRES, 1815–1914

Evelyn Bernette Ackerman

CORNELL UNIVERSITY PRESS
Ithaca and London

Cornell University Press gratefully acknowledges a grant from the Andrew W. Mellon Foundation that aided in bringing this book to publication.

First published 1978 by Cornell University Press.
Published in the United Kingdom by Cornell University Press Ltd.,
2–4 Brook Street, London W1Y 1AA.

International Standard Book Number 0-8014-1178-5
Library of Congress Catalog Card Number 78-58071
Printed in the United States of America
*Librarians: Library of Congress cataloging information appears
on the last page of the book.*

1-31-79

*To my parents
and to
the memory of
my grandparents*

Contents

Illustrations

Maps

Tables

Figure

Preface

On March 29, 1810, the empress Josephine, touring the countryside of the Ile-de-France, received the carefully prepared homage of many small towns along the main road from Paris to Normandy. Her intention was not to penetrate the life and workings of these villages of the Seine Valley; she had come to bring them a fleeting glimpse of imperial splendor. And in accordance with instructions received the day before from the subprefect of the region, their leading officials gathered together to present their respects.

Witness the scene in Bonnières, the main town of a canton in the department of the Seine-et-Oise. The mayor and his assistant in their official regalia, the justice of the peace and his clerk, the town councilors—all Bonnières's civic officialdom— assembled on the main highway, escorted by a contingent of the town's National Guard. The priest and his assistant, dressed in their sacerdotal vestments, positioned themselves at the doors of the church. Three hours later the empress Josephine, preceded by her police escort, arrived in a carriage drawn by eight horses. The civil officials bowed deeply, each in turn; the National Guardsmen presented arms and cried, "Long live the empress!" She graciously acknowledged the priests' greetings and then, escorted by the Bonnières and Mantes police, disappeared quickly from view.[1]

A rather wooden encounter, and one can almost sense the

[1]This episode is described in the ordinances of the mayor, entry of March 29, 1810. The ordinances of the mayor for the years after 1800 are preserved in the Archives Municipales de Bonnières.

disappointment in the town council's observations on the speed of her departure. The empress Josephine, to be sure, was no social historian or regional planner, but had she wanted to reflect upon the future development of one of the picturesque villages she saw that brisk March day, she would have done well to consider Bonnières.

This book examines the many transformations that took place in Bonnières between the end of the reign of Napoleon and the beginning of the First World War. My attention was first drawn to Bonnières by Marcel Delafosse, the chief archivist of the Archives Départementales des Yvelines, to whom I had written expressing my desire to study the modernization of a village in nineteenth-century France. For me, modernization meant industrialization, and Monsieur Delafosse, while apparently amused by what he called my very American tendency to equate the two, suggested the commune of Bonnières. Located on the left bank of the Seine River on the border of the Ile-de-France and Normandy, Bonnières had been a fairly important town in the river transport systems of the eighteenth century. During the nineteenth century, Bonnières's growth was favored by the establishment of a railway station on the Paris–Rouen line in 1843 and by the subsequent decision of one Jules Michaux to found his little industrial empire in the village. I happily set to work analyzing demographic change, industrial development, and social interaction.

From time to time I thought about Monsieur Delafosse's reaction to my initial premise that industrialization was a precondition of modernization. After all, communes that did not industrialize during the nineteenth century nonetheless managed to change in important ways. I began to view modernization as something that takes place on several levels, not the least important of which is the psychological. For a community to lose its tradition-bound peasant character, its members must have some minimum sense of autonomy, some confidence in their ability to influence and regulate the forces that affect them. I am speaking not about something as sophisticated as political change, but rather of such basic areas as control over one's own body. An early development in nineteenth-century Bonnières was the growth of this sense of self-determination, first in family planning and later in the management of health problems. By the end of the nineteenth century, the Bonnièrois did not view themselves as helpless in the face of natural forces, as did their ancestors in the early years of Napoleon's reign. Families could now be kept within reasonable size; doctors' opinions could be sought for health problems.

From this perspective, the development of nineteenth-century Bonnières becomes more understandable. Many of the changes that took place in the mentality of the nineteenth-century Bonnièrois occurred elsewhere also; birth control and vaccination, for example, spread throughout most of France. Bonnières is special because the mental transformations that took place in the town were accompanied, and certainly aided by, continued economic dynamism and expansion. Together these forces helped to bring Bonnières out of the rural, tradition-dominated matrix of the eighteenth century and into the fast-moving world of the twentieth.

A good part of this book is based on the classical techniques of historical demography. The French have refined demographic analysis so nicely that its use becomes almost imperative in a work that endeavors to penetrate the mentality of past populations. In this study, the vital records of Bonnières between 1736 and 1915 were analyzed according to the methods perfected by Louis Henry, and family reconstructions were made for all families formed from marriages that took place during that period.[2] To complement the information from the vital records, the well-preserved censuses of the nineteenth century were used. The first available census for the commune of Bonnières is that of 1817. After that, censuses are available for 1836 and for every fifth year thereafter except 1916, when no census was taken because of the First World War. For this study, the censuses of 1817, 1836, and every census thereafter taken in the sixth year of the decade up to and including 1906

[2]These methods, which are widely used by French demographic historians, are explained in Michel Fleury and Louis Henry, *Nouveau manuel de dépouillement et d'exploitation de l'état civil ancien* (Paris, 1965), and Louis Henry, *Manuel de démographie historique*, rev. ed. (Paris and Geneva, 1970).

were copied onto colored index cards, a different color for each census, a separate card for each household. Cards for families that recurred from census to census were clipped together in a modified patrilinear system.

The combination of census information and the vital records data made it possible to code an IBM card for each individual in post-1815 Bonnières, recording age, birthplace if known, residence within the commune, census years present, occupation, marital status, and information on spouse and spouse's family. Each card also contained information about number of children, nationality, servants residing within the household, age at death, and widowhood. A card was prepared for every individual who appeared on one of the censuses studied or who married such a person at Bonnières. Numerous passes of these 4,500 cards through the sorter yielded helpful information on migration, occupational structure, and household composition.

The other sources used in this book include materials from the Archives Municipales de Bonnières, the Archives Notariales de Bonnières, and the Archives Départementales des Yvelines. They are listed in the Bibliography.

I owe many debts of gratitude to the people who have helped me in my work on Bonnières. Without fear of indulging in undue sentimentality, I start the list of acknowledgments with my parents, Zelda and Arthur S. Ackerman, who taught me to speak French and to love France. I would also like to thank the teachers who introduced me to the rich world of French social history. David S. Landes encouraged my growing interest in historical demography, and was supportive and critical in just the right proportions. My interest in French village studies was greatly developed by courses, tutorials, and conversations with Laurence Wylie and Patrice L.-R. Higonnet, and by my wonderful years as a member of Professor Wylie's research team, studying the town of Chanzeaux in the department of the Maine-et-Loire.

This book was read in its entirety by Laurence Wylie, Victoria de Grazia, and Sanford Elwitt, who provided helpful criticisms. Dora B. Weiner generously shared with me her extensive knowledge of French medical history and commented on Chapter 1, as did Caroline Hannaway. Enid A. Lang, M.D., was a helpful and ready adviser. Bernhard Kendler and Barbara H. Salazar were patient and thorough editors. Thanks are also due to the History Department of Harvard University for generous financial support that allowed me to spend the year 1969–70 in France doing the preliminary research for this study, and to the Research Foundation of the City University of New York for a grant that enabled me to spend the summer of 1974 studying problems of public health in the Archives Départementales des Yvelines.

I am also grateful to many people on the other side of the Atlantic. I have already mentioned some of the ways in which Marcel Delafosse helped me to orient my work on Bonnières. I would also like to thank his efficient and pleasant staff. Marcel Lachiver, the reigning historian of the Mantes region and *maître-assistant* at the Sorbonne, shared with me his vast knowledge of the sources for the study of social history in the Yvelines. He has been cordially encouraging from the beginning of my work on Bonnières, meeting with me there and in Paris. Louis Chevalier of the Collège de France gave me excellent advice in sketching the broad outlines of this book when it was in its beginning stages. The people at the town hall and the notary's office of Bonnières have been patient and good friends. Françoise and Bernard de Oliveira, teachers at the Lycées Molière and Delacroix in Paris, did much to make my visits to France homecomings as well as research forays.

Finally, there is one man to whom my debt of gratitude is so great that it requires special explanation. Bonnières does not really need a historian, for it already has one in the person of Albert Anne. Head of Bonnières's Liberation Committee and mayor of the town from the end of the Second World War until 1964, Monsieur Anne has written many works on the Bonnières region, and it is thanks to him that the municipal archives are so rich and well organized. From the day of my arrival in Bonnières he unstintingly shared with me his vast knowledge of the history and traditions of his town. It is almost impossible to thank him adequately for his encouragement and advice.

Passages from Chapter 3 and the Afterword previously appeared in *French Historical Studies,* Spring 1977, in an article entitled "Alternative to Rural Exodus: The Development of the Commune of Bonnières-sur-Seine in the Nineteenth Century," and are reprinted here with the permission of the editor. Similarly, several pages from Chapter 1 first appeared in *Annales de démographie historique,* 1977, in an article entitled "The Commune of Bonnières-sur-Seine in the Eighteenth and Nineteenth Centuries," and are reprinted here with the permission of the editor.

E. B. A.

New York City

Village on the Seine

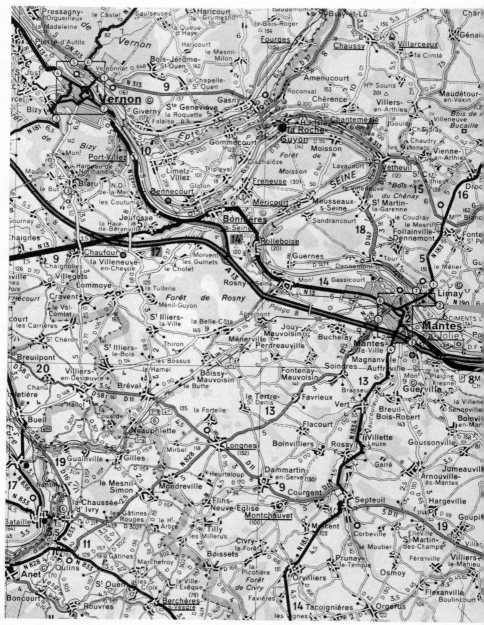

Bonnières and the surrounding countryside. From Michelin map no. 97, 16th ed., based on the topographical maps of the National Geographic Institute, Paris.

INTRODUCTION

Bonnières during the
Bourbon Restoration

The town of Bonnières lies nestled in a curve of the left bank
of the Seine River some forty-three miles northwest of Paris.
The village is part of the Mantois, the softly rolling countryside
surrounding the sleepy town of Mantes-la-Jolie. During the
nineteenth century, Mantes contained the subprefecture from
which the town council of Bonnières sought authorization to
repair its church steeple or to modify its budget, the hospital
where old people sometimes went to die, the thrice-weekly public markets where grain, vegetables, and animals changed
hands. Bonnières itself was the seat of the canton of Bonnières,
the most northwesterly canton of the department of the Seine-
et-Oise; today it is the biggest and richest commune of that
canton.[1] During the nineteenth century it often shared that
title with Bennecourt, its twin village on the opposite bank of
the Seine. Late-nineteenth-century developments, however,
primarily the expansion of industry, gave Bonnières ultimate
hegemony over Bennecourt.

Despite its industrial sector, Bonnières is an engagingly lovely
village, caught up as it is in one of the many sinuous curves of
the Seine. True, the seven villages that surround Bonnières—
Rosny, Rolleboise, Freneuse, Bennecourt, Jeufosse, La Ville-

[1]The boundaries of the departments of the Paris region were redrawn in
1964, and Bonnières is presently located in the recently created department of
the Yvelines. Since this study is about Bonnières before 1915, reference will be
made to the older department of the Seine-et-Oise. Similarly, although the
official name of Bonnières became Bonnières-sur-Seine in 1901, the town will
be referred to simply as Bonnières.

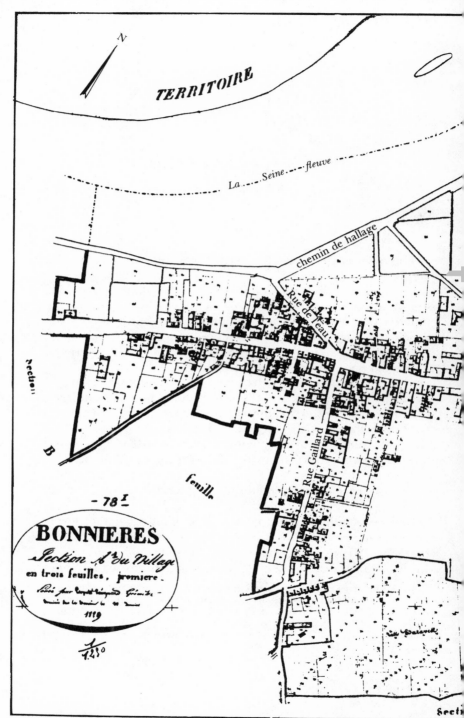

The bourg in 1829. Service du cadastre, Versailles

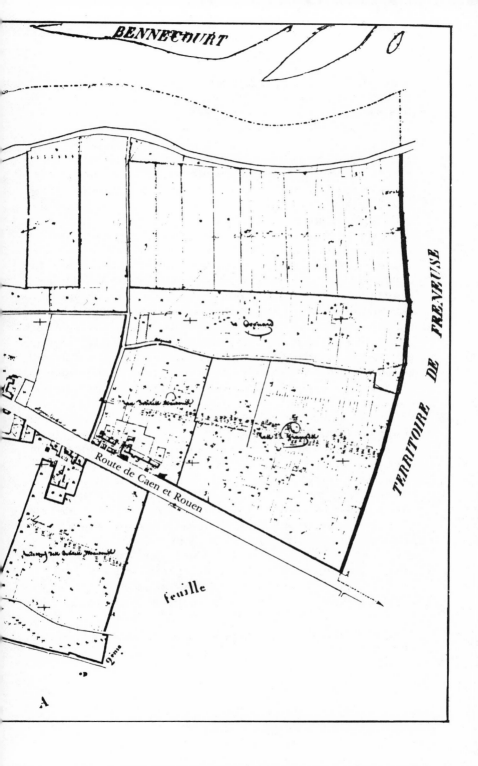

BENNECOURT

TERRITOIRE DE FRENEUSE

Route de Caen et Rouen

feuille

A

neuve-en-Chevrie, and Lommoye—have a more purely pastoral allure. Nonetheless, Bonnières has inspired its share of artists and writers. Paul Cézanne, for example, painted Bennecourt several times, and it has been said that he painted the church at Bonnières as well.[2] Jean Baptiste Corot, living in Rosny, also painted scenes of the Seine between Bonnières and Bennecourt. Emile Zola brought Bonnières into the mainstream of nineteenth-century French literature by using it in his novel *L'Oeuvre* as the prototype of a fresh country town set off against the bohemian squalor of his hero's Parisian art studio.

All this talk of bucolic charm might lead one to think that Bonnières lay quaintly isolated from the main arteries of transportation. Nothing could be further from the truth. Since the eighteenth century, Bonnières has been extremely well serviced by national roads. Bisected today by the Autoroute de Normandie, Bonnières in the nineteenth century was traversed by the major thoroughfare from Paris to Rouen, which formed the main street of the town. Bonnières was also crossed by a second highway, the road to Caen. The presence of these roads, as well as the Seine River, helped make Bonnières a strategic point in the land and water transportation systems of the prerailroad era.

A closer look at the commune itself reveals an agglomeration along the main street, which runs parallel to the Seine. This is the *bourg,* which at the beginning of the Bourbon Restoration contained the major part of the village's population, 534 people to be exact, or 73 percent of the total population of 727. A traveler entering Bonnières from Paris on his way to Rouen would have first noticed some scattered houses along the side of the road. On his left, he would have been struck by the fairly elaborate residence of Vincent Guillaume Foissy, the justice of the peace of the canton of Bonnières. Foissy was one of the minor notables of Restoration Bonnières, and although he surely would not have invited our hypothetical voyager to inspect his home, we are able to do so, thanks to the inventory of

[2]Rodolphe Walter, "Un Vrai Cézanne: 'La vue de Bonnières'," *Gazette des Beaux-Arts* 61 (1963): 359–366.

his belongings which was drawn up after his death in 1832.[3] Foissy's two-story residence, which he shared with his wife and three daughters, was among the more elaborate in Bonnières. His living room contained, in addition to the usual furnishings, such stylish extra touches as a massive clock on a tall black marble base and richly fringed curtains. In the sleeping alcove stood a lavish bed, worth four or five times as much as the bed in the average peasant dwelling, complete with goose-feather mattress and scarlet silk canopy. Not only was the Foissy house attractively furnished, both upstairs and down; it also bore the signs of some literacy and culture: twenty-four books, including three prayerbooks, and nine small portraits. The Foissys had come to Bonnières during the early years of Napoleon's reign from the town of Septeuil, eight miles to the south, and their association with Bonnières was fleeting. Their two oldest daughters married and left Bonnières; the youngest girl died in 1823. In their own way, the Foissys were typical Bonnièrois of the early nineteenth century; other members of the notable class in Bonnières also had comparatively brief associations with the village, and most of their children married outside it.

Next door to the Foissys, as we follow our traveler through Bonnières, were two families, both named Maloche, and both typical of another sort of Bonnièrois. Charles Antoine Maloche and his brother Jean Jacques were winegrowers who owned slightly more than two hectares apiece, sizable holdings for Bonnières farmers of the Restoration. Unlike the Foissy children, who married people from Mantes and Châteaudun, all the Maloche children remained in Bonnières after their marriage, often marrying colorful or important people in the village. Marie Catherine Maloche, Charles Antoine's daughter, married Pierre François Legrand, Bonnières's schoolteacher for a good quarter century, and Jean Jacques's granddaughter, Justine

[3] Archives Notariales de Bonnières, Fonds Rousselin. Notarial records are an excellent source of information on social history. Inventories compiled after death were the most helpful documents for this study, since they list all the furniture and possessions of the deceased, as well as outstanding debts. Marriage contracts, records of land sales and leases, and wills were also consulted. Since notarial archives are closed for a 125-year period, I was able to use them only for the years up to 1852.

Elisabeth Maloche, married Louis Leblond, a future mayor and industrial entrepreneur. We shall have occasion to meet the schoolteacher and the mayor again. Charles Antoine Maloche sat on the town council, as did Pierre Prosper Maloche, the youngest son of Jean Jacques.

Proceeding down the road, our traveler would pause at the home of Jean Etienne Claye, mayor of Bonnières and proprietor of the relay of post horses, the single most profitable enterprise in preindustrial Bonnières. Claye lived in a large house surrounded by three stables that contained the horses and equipment he needed for his business. In scale and complexity, the Claye house dwarfed all other Bonnières residences, even that of the justice of the peace. Not only did the Clayes have comfortable furniture; they had many distractions. To while away long evenings, they had their own gaming table and checkers table. A handsome marble-topped commode contained maps, atlases, and gambling equipment. As they amused themselves with these items, the Clayes sipped coffee from porcelain cups or drank wine from crystal glasses, luxuries no other family in Bonnières could match. Their four bedrooms were elegant: expensive goose-down-filled beds covered with counterpanes of *toile de Jouy;* some of their rooms even featured wall coverings of toile de Jouy. Not surprisingly, the Clayes were satisfied with the established political order; their house was decorated with fifteen pictures of the royal family and a bust of the king. Their only daughter, Marie Natalie, was pampered; alone among Bonnières children she had ten dresses, some of them in the toile de Jouy the Clayes evidently favored, others in cotton.

As our traveler continued into Bonnières, he would come up to old Madame Saunier's inn on his right. One of the many inns and cafés in the Bonnières of the prerailroad era, this establishment doubtless achieved special notoriety in the 1840s, when Madame Saunier's daughter-in-law Sophie Varin, from the neighboring town of Rosny, posed for Corot when he needed a pretty model for the Virgin Mary in his painting *The Flight into Egypt.* But this was in the future, and during the Restoration Saunier's inn had plenty of competition from other hostels in Bonnières, establishments we shall examine in more detail later.

Right next to Saunier's inn stood Bonnières's church, an undistinguished building erected in 1740 originally as an auxiliary chapel to the main church in the hamlet of Mesnil Resnard.[4] And diagonally opposite the church was the large, sprawling home and farm buildings of Jean Antoine Langlois, Bonnières's largest landowner according to the 1829 cadastre, its unofficial schoolteacher for some thirty years, and a major winegrower in the town.

Jean Antoine Langlois must have been an interesting character. He was born in the neighboring town of Lommoye to farmer parents, but he was a resident of Bonnières at the time of his marriage in 1798. To the people of Bonnières he was a man of undisputed erudition. When Langlois tried to sign up for the National Guard at the time of the Revolution, local tradition has it, his friends dissuaded him, saying, "Our duty is at the frontier—yours is here, in your school. Stay there, you will read to our parents the letters we will write them from the army camps of the Republic. Your skilled pen will write down their answers for us."[5] Now, Jean Antoine Langlois certainly was a lettered man. He served as town clerk, and he signed his name repeatedly in the vital records registers in a fine, flowing hand. Two of his brothers were also schoolteachers. Yet it is instructive to note that a third brother was a simple linen weaver, and Langlois's own bride was unable to sign her name. Literacy, evidently, was a very chancy thing in the early-nineteenth-

[4]The commune of Bonnières, established legally after the Revolution, corresponded to the former parish of Mesnil Resnard. At the beginning of the eighteenth century, Mesnil Resnard had a larger population than Bonnières, and therefore housed the main church. The construction of the roads to Rouen and Caen via Bonnières between 1738 and 1753, however, stimulated demographic growth in Bonnières, so by the beginning of the nineteenth century its population exceeded that of Mesnil Resnard, and it was more logical to designate Bonnières as the administrative seat of the former parish of Mesnil Resnard.

[5]Quoted in Maurice Poncelet, *Histoire de la Ville de Bonnières-sur-Seine* (Mantes, 1947), p. 102, n. 2. Poncelet's monograph on Bonnières is enlivened by several such quotes, passed down over the generations in Bonnières. This translation, and all others, are mine.

century countryside. Jean Antoine Langlois must have poured all his hopes into his son Antoine Sulpice; he surely had him well educated, for by the 1820s, Antoine Sulpice was a notary's clerk. But the young man died in 1828, three years after Langlois's daughter Marie Rosalie married a jeweler and accompanied him to Paris. Their daughter would eventually return to Bonnières to marry Jules Michaux, the man who was to transform the town's economy during the Second Empire. But this, too, lies in the future. Let us leave Jean Antoine Langlois in his large home, teaching his pupils, tending his ten hectares of vines, fulfilling his duties as town clerk, and continue our trek down the main street of Bonnières.

Once we have passed the church, the main street, called simply the Grande Rue, still stretches out long before us. The houses and shops of artisans dot this road: Gilles Etienne Sembat, the cobbler; Grégoire Chatelain, the cloth merchant; René David, the mason; Pierre Jean Baptiste Ovièvre, the harness maker; Charles François Pommier, the baker. The commercial life of Bonnières was centered on this main road; the second principal street of the village, the rue Gaillard, led south from it toward the hamlets. Many Bonnières winegrowers lived on the rue Gaillard and on the small lanes branching off from it. Were we to follow the rue Gaillard, it would lead us toward the geographical center of the commune, toward the six hamlets of Bonnières: Mesnil Resnard, Le Clos Esnault, Morvent, Les Guinets, La Boissière, and Champ Pin Baillet. These hamlets followed the pattern of most nineteenth-century rural hamlets dependent on bourgs; three of them were to shrink greatly, and three of them, Le Clos Esnault, La Boissière, and Champ Pin Baillet, were to disappear by the eve of the First World War.

The people of Bonnières busied themselves at three principal occupations in 1815: winegrowing, woodcutting and general farming, and river and overland transportation. Of the 193 people in the active work force in 1817, the year of the first nominative census, 57, or about 30 percent, were occupied with the cultivation of vines. Jean Baptiste Bonnecourt, for example, lived on the main street but left it every morning to

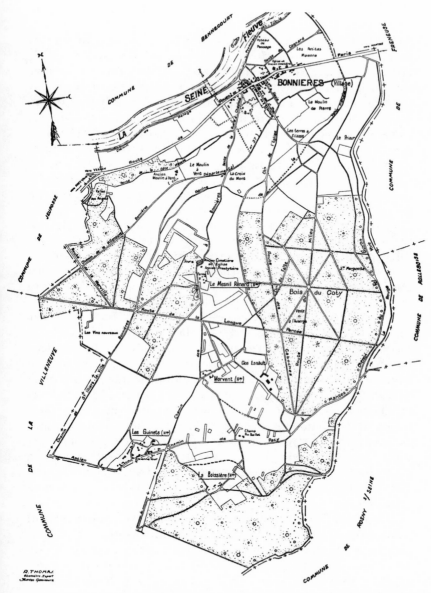

The bourg and the hamlets in 1829. From Maurice Poncelet, *Histoire de la ville de Bonnières-sur-Seine* (Mantes, 1947).

tend the two scattered hectares of vines he owned in various parts of the commune. Jean Denis, too, left his small dwelling off the rue Gaillard each day to work in his somewhat smaller vineyards. Winegrowing, however, was beginning to decline as the mainstay of Bonnières's agriculture in the early part of the nineteenth century; its heyday had been seventy years before, when fully one-third of the township had been covered with vines and more than half the work force was employed in their cultivation. The vineyards took up the middle section of the village, sandwiched between the rich land near the river in the northern part of town and the woods belonging to the large noble estate at the southern end of the village.

Woodcutters, small farmers, and a few agricultural day laborers accounted for another sizable part of the work force, forty people, or about 20 percent of the active population, according to the census of 1817. The heavily wooded southern portion of Bonnières, where the woodcutters lived, belonged to the estate of the duchess of Berry. Though she lived in Rosny, the duchess was by far the largest landholder in Bonnières; her 326-hectare estate accounted for almost half of the village's territory. Her actual participation in the life of the hamlets, however, appears to have been minimal. The Boursiers and the Bouviers, for example, woodcutters and mainstays of the small hamlet of La Boissière, probably never saw her and dealt only briefly with her agent when it was time to renegotiate their leases. In Les Guinets, the largest hamlet, twelve farmers and woodcutters toiled on her land, and even a few artisans lived there, but these were the artisans of poverty: a sole weaver, a deaf-mute tailor whose scanty personal effects, when inventoried in 1842, must inspire pity in even the most dispassionate historian.

It was the occupations connected with river and overland transportation that gave Restoration Bonnières much of its special flavor. Sixteen percent of the work force in 1817 was directly or indirectly involved in providing transportation services, or with furnishing food and lodging for those who provided such services. Louis Hippolyte Lorion, for example, had a boat that he moored at the nearby port of Rolleboise; Jean Pierre Chatelain made his living as a carriage driver. François Napoléon Dutois, the parish priest of Bonnières between 1845 and 1870 and author of an excellent monograph about the town, provided many details of the activities that flourished at the beginning of the century:

A considerable number of people lived solely through the operation of the relay of horses, cartage of merchandise, and navigation. Seventeen stagecoaches and several carriages traveling to Evreux, Vernon, Louviers, and Les Andelys crossed the countryside every day. The merchandise sent by overland carriages arriving on the Rouen and Caen roads or going to destinations in Normandy, the animals going to Poissy caused a round-the-clock bustle of activity and employed a considerable number of people who were unfamiliar with jobs other than riding a horse, steering a boat, climbing a riverbank, leading oxen, drinking and gambling while waiting for more business.[6]

The abbé Dutois continued in his monograph to write nostalgically of the climate of *dolce far niente* which prevailed in Bonnières before the coming of the railroad. Indeed, if one may judge by the number of inns and cafés in Restoration Bonnières, there must have been a great variety of ways in which Louis Hippolyte Lorion, Jean Pierre Chatelain, and their colleagues could pass the time. Charles Chevalier, for example, owned a café on the main street of Bonnières, at the entrance to the village, just opposite Jean Antoine Langlois's house. What went on in his café? Perhaps lively arguments, for Chevalier's nickname was Frondeur (Bickerer). We can speculate with more information at hand about the activities in François Crot's inn, farther down the main street. Unlike Chevalier, François Crot was not a native Bonnièrois. Born in Mantes in 1798, he was the son of a blacksmith from the Côte-d'Or who had evidently done a bit of traveling. Crot's parents must have witnessed at least some of the intense action of the Revolution, for Crot had a brother born in Paris in 1792. By 1795 his parents

---

[6] François Napoléon Dutois, *"Monographie de Bonnières,"* ca. 1860, in the Archives Départementales des Yvelines (hereafter cited as ADY). Albert Anne has prepared a typewritten transcription of this manuscript which he was kind enough to lend me. The pages are not numbered.

had fled the excitement of the capital and moved to the department of the Calvados. It is easy to imagine Crot's café in the early 1820s, with Old Man Crot regaling the assembled drinkers with elaborate stories of Paris during the time of L'Incorruptible.

The other innkeepers of Bonnières may not have been able to compete with Crot's repertory of revolutionary stories, but their cafés had other attractions. Gambling seems to have been popular among both Bonnièrois and travelers passing through. Half the rooms at the widow Tavernier's rather elaborately furnished inn had their own gaming tables. A more public gambling arrangement was a feature of Jean Pierre Mouchard's café, which boasted a separate gaming room with a fully equipped billiard table. Several café owners had equipment for *tamis,* the croquet-like game popular in the Mantois. At Raffy's inn and also *chez* Joseph Gosselin, the people of Bonnières could rent the wooden frame strung with catgut and the small white balls with which this game was played.[7]

The boatmen and carriage drivers who assembled at François Crot's café or Raffy's inn were not the only nonagricultural workers in Bonnières. Restoration Bonnières had its complement of artisans: cobblers, tailors, masons, agricultural artisans. And finally, in keeping with its position as the head of a canton, Bonnières had a sprinkling of local officials: Justice of the Peace Vincent Guillaume Foissy, a court clerk, tax officials, a bureaucrat who worked at the subprefecture in Mantes. The priest, a notary, and several merchants rounded out the meager roster of cadres in 1817 Bonnières society.

Who were these people, how did they live, where were they from? Two out of every three villagers in 1817 had been born in Bonnières, and most of the remaining Bonnièrois were of local origin, natives of one of the seven contiguous villages or of some other town within the canton. Their physical and social environment was described in copious detail by Armand Cassan, the subprefect of the arrondissement of Mantes dur-

[7]For a description of *tamis,* see M. Tercinet, "Le Jeu de tamis dans le Mantois," *Le Mantois* 4 (1953):16–17.

ing the 1820s.[8] For this population, of which Cassan was una-
bashedly very fond, youth was very brief, covering the years
between nineteen and twenty-five for men and seventeen and
twenty for women. The Bonnièrois were not tall; the most
frequently encountered heights ranged between five feet and
five feet three inches. Here is Cassan's description of the
physical appearance of the people of the area: "The young
men of the cantons of Limay and Bonnières are short and
thickset; their features are prominent, their facial expressions
active; the women are of average height, well built, alert, active, industrious."[9]

The living conditions in Bonnières appear adequate, perhaps
even good for the period, but to our minds lacking in comfort.
Most people ate four or five meals in the summertime: two
breakfasts, one at four in the morning and the second at eight;
dinner at noon; a hearty snack at four or five in the afternoon;
and supper at nine or ten in the evening. In the winter one
meal was eliminated and supper came at seven in the evening.
Cassan provided a detailed description of the diet of a farmer
in the Mantois: "His breakfast consists of bread and cheese; his
dinner is soup, sometimes with meat in it, and some cheese and
fruit; his snack is bread and cheese; his supper is the same soup
he had at dinner, which was put in his bed and covered with
the pillow to keep it warm, and also a salad with a lot of vinegar
and a little bit of oil."[10]

This diet appears deficient in protein and low in calories as
well, at least for a man engaged in farmwork. Cassan was of the
opinion that the average diet in the Mantois was somewhat
lacking in meat. The question of meat consumption among the
agricultural classes has always excited interest, yet an idea of
the amount of meat eaten must remain only approximate.[11]

[8]Armand Cassan, *Statistique de l'arrondissement de Mantes* (Mantes, 1833). Cassan's study is intelligently conceived and well documented. It is an essential
source for any historian of the Mantes region in the early nineteenth century.
Many similar studies were done by local officials of the time; Cassan's work is
one of the better ones.
[9]Ibid., p. 37.
[10]Ibid., p. 43.
[11]Guy Thuillier, who has done exhaustive research on living conditions in the

Cassan observed that beef, veal, and lamb were eaten only in times of illness or on a feast day; mutton was eaten during the month of November because it was relatively cheap then. But usually, Cassan asserted, when the farmer in the Mantes region ate meat, it was salt pork, for by the early 1820s each family had a pig. This would seem a reasonable assessment of the situation in Bonnières, for Martin Anfray, the sole butcher in the town, could not have supplied meat to more than two hundred households on a regular basis.

The farmer's idea of a regal spread reflects the modesty of his expectations: a fricasseed rabbit, a salad accompanied by hard-boiled eggs or cream, blood sausage, pork sausage, slices of grilled fatback, a large biscuit made of flour and salt and served with or without lard. The usual bread was of whole meal, a mixture of rye and barley or wheat and rye, or a combination of all three grains. Cassan viewed it as an improvement over the daily bread of the prerevolutionary period, which was often pure barley, mixed sometimes with oats. Cider and less often wine—diluted with water—were the usual beverages.

Thus the diet of the Mantois farmer was Spartan, and so was his lodging. The elements of style and comfort present in the Foissy and Claye homes at the entrance to Bonnières were not to be found in most winegrowers' dwellings. Jean Pierre Bonnecourt, the winegrower from the main street whom we have already met, lived in the more typical arrangement well described by Cassan:

The country dweller's home is generally only a single room containing a bed, a closet, a breakfront for dishes, a table, buckets, stewing pots, frying pans, chairs, children's cradles, and so forth. When this room is large and belongs to a wealthy farmer, a plaster or wooden screen divides it into two unequal parts, the smaller of which serves as a room for the children. In addition to the main house, each family has a cellar or storeroom for its wine and beverages, potatoes, turnips; a

Nivernais, writes in *Aspects de l'économie nivernaise au XIX* siècle (Paris, 1966): "Our uncertainty as regards the consumption of meat is . . . great. It is traditionally asserted that peasants and workers eat no meat, except on holidays or during the season of heavy work, and that they ordinarily eat only the meat of their pig—when they have one" (pp. 49–50).

barn, often vaulted and underground; a stable, a place for the pig, a chicken coop—all this is enhanced by a yard and a garden.[12]

Cassan, viewing the quality of housing in the Mantois, saw a decided improvement after 1790, and even more marked progress after 1810 or so. During the eighteenth century, houses often had thin walls, a single small window referred to as an *oeil-de-boeuf* (bull's-eye), and thatched roofs; houses of more recent construction, on the other hand, had large windows bordered with quarry stones and tiled roofs. Housing in the canton of Bonnières was among the best in the arrondissement. Thatch-roofed homes, for example, were relatively rare in the Bonnières area, and those that existed were well constructed. Yet despite this comparative superiority, much of the housing in Bonnières was far from adequate or even healthful. The quarters of Jean Pierre Bonnecourt were clearly separated from those of his animals (a calf and an ass), but poorer Bonnièrois lived in closer proximity to their stock. This situation seems to have been more prevalent in the hamlets than in the bourg, suggesting a different standard of living in these two parts of Bonnières.

The cultural life, or what the French would call the moral life, of Bonnières around 1820 is much more difficult to assess. According to Louis Anquetin, a schoolmaster in late-nineteenth-century Bonnières, schools were established toward the end of the seventeenth century and maintained without serious interruption until 1833, when the Guizot law obligated all French communes to establish primary schools.[13] This tradition is probably one reason that literacy in Restoration Bonnières was relatively high, at least among men; more than three out of every four young men who married in the town were capable of signing their names. Female literacy was much lower; at the beginning of the Restoration, fewer than half the brides in Bonnières could sign their names. Anquetin observed that "the

[12]Cassan, *Statistique,* p. 40.
[13]Louis Anquetin, "Monographie de Bonnières" (ADY). Anquetin's manuscript was prepared for the Exposition of 1900. All the schoolteachers in France were asked to write sketches of their communities for the exposition, and their writings remain one of the great unused sources of information on nineteenth-century French life.

need to know how to read and do basic business arithmetic must doubtless have been felt in this town of innkeepers, carriage drivers, stagecoach drivers, and boatmen who were in constant contact with travelers."[14] As proof, Anquetin pointed to the higher literacy rates observed in the bourg, where transportation workers and shopkeepers lived, in comparison with the hamlets, peopled mainly by winegrowers and woodcutters.

Granted that male literacy in Bonnières was comparatively good, there is still a long way to go from signing one's name to reading a book. Except for such notables as the Clayes and the Foissys and the successive bailiffs, few Bonnièrois owned books. The prevailing attitude toward "book culture" can be glimpsed in the cursory way they were inventoried: "five unmatched volumes"; "twenty volumes, some bound and some unbound." The libraries of three men were inventoried in detail; since they were all in the legal profession, many of their books were predictable: *Le Parfait Notaire, Les Coutumes de Mantes et Meulan,* and the like. Louis Victor Celles, a bailiff who died in 1837, alone owned any literary works to speak of: a sixty-seven-volume set of the writings of Voltaire, the letters of Madame de Sévigné, the works of Montesquieu, Montaigne, and Boileau. Whether he had read them is another matter. Certainly we cannot speak of a rich literary culture among any group in Bonnières society in the first half of the nineteenth century.

Nor was a strong Catholic faith a feature of Bonnières life at that time. The Mantois had never been thoroughly evangelized, and Bonnières seems to have been no exception. The notables' support of the church during the Restoration did not alter the basic trend away from it; the abbé Dutois pointed out that the Feugère family, prominent during the eighteenth century and intermarried with the Clayes during the early nineteenth, contributed greatly to the restoration of the church after the Revolution. When this very devout family left Bonnières in 1820, Dutois noted, the number of people fulfilling their Easter duty began to decline. In a more general cultural way, however, the church remained an important part

14Ibid., p. 158.

of village life, and several times a year the streets were filled
with colorful processions on major feast days. Each April 25,
for example, on the Feast of St. Mark, the people and clergy
walked to the mission cross at Morvent, and on the three Roga-
tion days preceding Ascension, forty days after Easter, processions wound through the fields of the village as blessings were
asked for the crops. And again on August 15, after vespers had
been said on Assumption Day, a procession filled the streets of
the bourg. Several Bonnières families possessed religious objects, and women of modest means often had as their sole piece
of jewelry a gold cross, which traditionally served as an engage-
ment gift in the Mantois. A few households had religious books
and the Foissys owned a missal, carefully stored in a tooled
leather box.

Such, then, was the material and cultural life of the town
around the year 1815. Basically a farming village—well over half
the work force was engaged in agriculture—it contained a population whose day-to-day existence, while improved over what it
had been in the eighteenth century, included few luxuries. Meager eating habits had made disease and death an ever present
reality; Cassan pointed to pleurisy, pneumonia, and inflamma-
tory diseases in general as the chief maladies of the region.[15]
Although Bonnières was comparatively well connected with the
outside world, its population was almost exclusively made up of
men and women from the immediate region.

This is how the historian views the Bonnières of the early
nineteenth century. How the people of the village viewed it can
best be seen through their own words. On the one hand, the
mayor installed in 1828 declared that he knew that want was
great in the area, and promised to do what he could to alleviate
it. But the petition that the town council sent to the subprefect
of Mantes in 1808 asking for permission to establish a public
market on Mondays and an annual fair on the Monday before
Easter revealed great pride in the primacy of the village in
relation to the surrounding towns, in its peaceful atmosphere
favorable to commerce, and in its resources. To be sure, this

[15]Cassan, *Statistique*, p. 37. One should not, of course, put too much faith in
Cassan's diagnoses. Pleurisy, for example, could have been tuberculosis.

pride was at least in part a matter of local patriotism, but the
town council of Bonnières pointed out that

for as long as anyone can remember, people from the neighboring
communes have been coming daily to sell their goods in our town
because of [its] large population, its thickly populated bourg, its excellent communications, either by the first-rate main highways that meet
at Bonnières and the good local roads or by the Seine, on which
Bonnières has a port. In addition, Bonnières [has had] a relay of
horses and a postal service for as long as anyone can remember. Finally, merchants and farmers would find great security and protection
in Bonnières's public market because in addition to the town hall, it
has a justice of the peace and a brigade of imperial police who are
often reinforced by extra detachments when the volume of traffic in
the town requires it. To all these advantages should be added the
peacefulness and love of order that its inhabitants have always
shown.[16]

Had the councilors of 1808 revisited their town a century
later, they would have felt their confidence in Bonnières vindi-
cated as they surveyed its busy factories and its many different
stores. They might have felt some pride, too, in the fact that
Bonnières had grown—from the 700-odd people of their day
to more than 1,200 souls—while the population of many of the
surrounding villages had declined.

[16]Archives Municipales de Bonnières, minutes of the town council meeting of
December 14, 1808.

CHAPTER 1

Demographic Change: Biological and Sentimental Components

During the Old Regime and at the beginning of the nineteenth century, the people of Bonnières lived in a close relationship with nature. The seasonal agricultural tasks shaped the calendar of marriages and, to a lesser degree, of births. Among infants and young children, mortality was regularly high. Periodic epidemics of scarlet fever, typhoid, and dysentery brought fear and death to the peasants of the Bonnières region, as they had to their ancestors.

Throughout the nineteenth century, the Bonnièrois remained to a very great extent in the grip of natural forces that they understood imperfectly and over which they had little control. But Restoration Bonnièrois also showed signs of an increasing ability to take steps to shape their own lives. Among those signs were the rapid diffusion of the practice of birth control after the Revolution of 1789, the virtual elimination of smallpox, and a perceptible decline in maternal childbirth-related deaths. Of course, as the French say, "Il ne faut pas exagérer": life expectancy did not rise significantly between 1816 and 1915, and infectious disease still claimed many lives. Nonetheless, in the two discrete areas of the control of smallpox and safer confinements, progress, perhaps more important psychologically than statistically, was made, and the Bonnièrois gained confidence in the possibilities of formal medicine. In addition, the century between 1816 and 1915 brought changes in their sentimental world; the church and the soil relaxed their holds on people's private lives as Bonnières became in-

creasingly secular and industrialized. Decisions about marriage
and sex, previously tailored to the requirements of the church
or the exigencies of the agricultural year, were more frequently
made for personal reasons alone as the nineteenth century
wore on. Feelings about children became transformed, and
centuries-old patterns of dealing with the very young were
modified in response to new emotional realities.

The first major change in the demographic behavior of the
people of postrevolutionary Bonnières was the rapid spread of
contraception.[1] Since the Revolution of 1789, increasing numbers of married couples in Bonnières had been turning toward
the regular practice of birth control, mirroring trends found
throughout the Mantois, and the region of Normandy and the
Ile-de-France generally.[2] Between 1756 and 1785 the average
size of a completed family in Bonnières had been 5.6 children,
but during the following thirty-year period, 1786–1815, the
average fell to 3.9 children, and by the time of the constitutional monarchy, 1816–1845, completed family size in Bonnières was down to 2.9.[3] Couples in the 1840s in other words,
were having roughly half as many children as their ancestors a
century earlier.

Explaining a general collective switch to restrained fertility is
a difficult task. Economic, sociopolitical, religious, and psycho-

[1] For a general discussion of contraception in France, see John T. Noonan,
Jr., *Contraception* (Cambridge, Mass., 1965), pp. 387–394, and Hélène Bergues
et al., *La Prévention des naissances dans la famille: Ses origines dans les temps modernes* (Paris, 1960). The contraceptive method employed by most French
couples in the late eighteenth and most of the nineteenth centuries was coitus
interruptus.

[2] For other examples of postrevolutionary decline in fertility in villages of
Normandy and the Ile-de-France, see Etienne Gautier and Louis Henry, *La
Population de Crulai, paroisse normande: Etude historique* (Paris, 1958), pp. 118–
120; Jean Ganiage, *Trois villages de l'Ile-de-France: Etude démographique* (Paris,
1963), p. 114; and Marcel Lachiver, *La Population de Meulan du XVIIe au XIXe
siècle (vers 1600–1870): Etude de démographie historique* (Paris, 1969), p. 165.
Marcel Lachiver's general article "Fécondité légitime et contraception dans la
région parisienne," in *Hommage à Marcel Reinhard: Sur la population française au
XVIIIe et au XIXe siècles*, ed. Jacques Dupâquier (Paris, 1973), pp. 383–401, is
also useful, especially pp. 395–396.

[3] Demographers traditionally use the number of children per completed
family as a measure of the fertility of a population. A completed family is one in
which both parents lived as a couple until the wife passed the age of forty-five.

logical factors all come into play in a complicated and interrelated fashion that virtually assures that any explanation advanced can only be a tentative one. It is fairly easy to point to several things that did not happen in Bonnières. The late eighteenth and early nineteenth centuries, for example, witnessed no decline in the rate of infant mortality which might have made parents feel less pressure to produce many children in order to ensure the survival of at least a few.[4] Nor is there any evidence suggesting a change in the legal or economic system in Bonnières between 1786 and 1815 which would have made it more advantageous for people to have smaller families. Well before the Revolution and Napoleon abolished primogeniture, Bonnières families had been dividing up property and wealth more or less equally among all children. The late eighteenth-century Bonnièrois were grain- and grape-producing farmers who owned minuscule amounts of land and rented more. Economically, small families would have been as great an advantage in the 1770s as they were in the 1820s, and indeed, a small percentage of Bonnières families must have resorted to birth control in the thirty years before 1790, if we are to judge by the spacing of their children. Yet it was only after the Revolution that many Bonnièrois began deliberately to limit the size of their families.

It certainly appears as though the decade of revolutionary turmoil had a deep effect on many Bonnièrois, especially on the cohort that reached marriageable age in the years between 1790 and 1815.[5] These people, influenced by the rapid succession of revolutionary events, in an era when the only constant was continual flux and upheaval, began to be emboldened to use their own initiative to make certain decisions in areas where they had hitherto obeyed church laws. Because of the imper-

---

[4]Infant mortality—that is, mortality of children less than one year old—declined only slightly between the periods 1766–1815 and 1816–1865. In the first fifty-year period, the infant mortality rate was 188 deaths per thousand births, and in the second it was 151 deaths per thousand births.

[5]This idea is developed by Emmanuel Le Roy Ladurie in "Démographie et 'funestes secrets': Le Languedoc (fin XVIIIe–début XIXe siècle)," *Annales historiques de la révolution française* 37 (1965):385–400, especially p. 399; and by Louis Henry in "L'Apport des témoignages et de la statistique," in Bergues et al., *Prévention des naissances* (Paris, 1960), pp. 361–376, especially p. 366.

fect evangelization of the Mantois, the church in the eighteenth century had received respect largely because of its association with the monarchy; when the church was disestablished during the Revolution, its authority may well have come to seem less imposing to the Bonnièrois, most of whom supported the Revolution. And even before the "dethroning" of the church, the Bonnièrois had watched their parish priest, Henri Martin, struggle to decide whether to take the oath to the Nation; his willingness to take it could only have reinforced the notion that all authority was being questioned, reformed, and reconceived. In many ways, the ten years following the outbreak of the Revolution can be seen as a sort of miniature Enlightenment for the common man. People in Bonnières had watched men in power experiment with different governmental forms during the 1790s; now, in a much quieter but no less revolutionary way, men and women began to question many of the traditional church teachings that affected them most intimately, the guidelines on marriage and the family. A young woman who married in 1804 at the age of twenty-two had spent her teen years, the time when her ideas on family and sexuality were formed, during the 1790s. She and her husband had come to maturity during a period when critical thought was the rule. They might well have been more inclined to decide for themselves what constituted a serious sin than a couple that had formed its basic attitudes in the quieter, more certain years before 1789.

This readjustment of attitudes is hardly a total rejection of the church, much less of Christianity, whose rites and festivals continued to punctuate life in Bonnières throughout the nineteenth century. Yet it certainly is a step away from the church's authority. Nor was the prohibition on contraception the only church teaching on marriage with which the Bonnièrois of the postrevolutionary period disagreed. The church had traditionally discouraged marriages during Lent and Advent, but after 1793 increasing numbers of Bonnièrois disregarded these guidelines. There were more March and December marriages in Bonnières during the 1790s than there had been during the entire five and a half decades between 1736 and 1790; one almost has the impression that people went out of their way to prove a point. Not all church strictures were rejected, however, for the villagers of the 1790–1815 period were not rabid anti-clericals. Concerned primarily with working out a more livable relationship with the church, the Bonnièrois continued to follow those of its dictates that they deemed good. The number of illegitimate births, for example, had been low before the Revolution and increased only slightly during the first half of the nineteenth century.

What the 1790s made possible in Bonnières was the development of a certain sense of autonomy and internalized self-control. The profound and widely publicized questioning of all political givens—and of many social and economic givens too—inspired the Bonnièrois to develop a disciplined freedom and independence in their private lives. There is something very modern about this picture of peasants, many of them illiterate and unschooled, finding in the years of revolutionary activity a lesson they could profitably apply to their personal lives. This image of the Bonnièrois of 1810 as people confidently facing the future, liberated from their old taboos, fades, however, when their reactions to other changes of the 1790–1830 period are considered.

Take, for example, their skeptical reaction to the attempts made by health and administrative authorities to introduce smallpox vaccination. The story of these efforts is instructive, for in it we can trace the stages by which the Bonnièrois accepted a medical innovation. In retrospect, their initial reluctance to accept vaccination seems ironic, for the vaccination campaign of the first three decades of the nineteenth century eventually paid off handsomely, especially for children between the ages of thirteen months and four years. The mortality rate in this age group fell dramatically during the century between 1816 and 1915, from 139 deaths per thousand in 1816–1825 to 24 per thousand in 1896–1905. Put another way, whereas one out of every seven burials in the Bonnières cemetery between 1816 and 1825 was that of a young child, by the 1896–1905

period, only one out of every twenty-nine burials in Bonnières
was that of a youngster between the ages of thirteen months
and four years.[6] Much of this progress was due to improved
nutrition among the young, with a resulting decrease in deaths
from infectious diseases, especially the diarrheal diseases, but
another factor was the elimination of smallpox from the countryside.[7] Indeed, the successful war against smallpox was one of
the few real medical breakthroughs to affect the lives of the
French peasantry during the nineteenth century.

With the virtual disappearance of plague from Europe in the
first quarter of the eighteenth century, smallpox replaced it in
the popular mind as an object of fear. Viral in origin and
highly infectious, smallpox often disfigured those of its victims
it did not kill. Various forms of inoculation against smallpox
had been practiced since ancient times, but all of them involved
the absorption of live smallpox germs by the individual, an
inherently dangerous procedure. For this reason, Edward Jenner's discovery in 1798 that the less malignant cowpox germ
could immunize human beings against smallpox was greeted
warmly. By 1801, Jenner's work was receiving much publicity
in French medical and administrative circles. In April of that
year, for example, the subprefect of the arrondissement of
Mantes sent a circular to the mayors of all the communes in his
jurisdiction in which he detailed Jenner's work. Together with
other officials in the department of the Seine-et-Oise, he sponsored large outdoor vaccination ceremonies; his own grand-

[6]Juvenile mortality refers to the deaths of children aged thirteen months to
four years. The distinction between infant (under twelve months) and juvenile
mortality corresponds to an immunological as well as a chronological reality.
Infants are protected from certain diseases by antibodies that they receive from
their mothers; older children are not. Smallpox, for example, rarely hit infants
under one year of age, but after the first birthday it was a real threat.

[7]The importance of improved nutrition in reducing juvenile mortality is
discussed in Thomas McKeown, *The Modern Rise of Population* (New York and
San Francisco, 1976), p. 138. For the background on smallpox, see George
Rosen, *A History of Public Health* (New York, 1958), pp. 183–191; Cyril William
Dixon, *Smallpox* (London, 1962), pp. 187–295; William L. Langer, "Immuniza-
tion against Smallpox before Jenner," *Scientific American,* January 1976,
pp.112–117, especially p. 112; and Marcel Lachiver's review of my dissertation
("Bonnières-sur-Seine au XIXe ou les voies de l'industrialisation et de la crois-
sance démographique") in *Etudes de la région parisienne* 49 (1975):41–42.

daughter was one of the first children to be publicly vaccinated at Mantes.[8] Within several years, courses were set up to teach health professionals how to vaccinate; a poster dated January 28, 1805, announced such a course to be given weekly at the hospital of Versailles.

Doctors, *officiers de santé* (health officers),[9] and midwives must have availed themselves of the free instruction, for by the early 1820s a vaccination campaign was under way in the Bonnières region. Deaths from smallpox declined dramatically; 1816, a year when smallpox was rampant, saw 378 cases of smallpox, resulting in 68 deaths in the arrondissement of Mantes; but except for 1826 and 1827, when the disease reappeared in epidemic form, smallpox rarely claimed more than five lives a year after 1825.[10] A small army of medical personnel went around the Mantois vaccinating; lists of vaccinators drawn up in 1826 and 1827 show thirty to thirty-five doctors, officiers de santé, and midwives involved in this activity.

In spite of the great effectiveness of the vaccine, proved again and again in laboratories in Paris and in Passy, many peasants remained unconvinced and extremely uncomfortable about the injection of foreign substances into their bodies. Testimonies to this effect poured in to the subprefect at Mantes

[8]Archives Départementales des Yvelines (hereafter cited as ADY), 7 M 78. The subprefect described the public vaccination to the mayors of the communes of the arrondissement of Mantes in a circular of April 18, 1801, in an attempt to promote the idea of vaccination. The idea of public vaccination to allay popular fears has its origins in the eighteeenth century. In 1721 Lady Mary Wortley Montagu, the wife of the British ambassador to Constantinople, had her young son inoculated against smallpox in Turkey. When she returned to England later that year, she had her daughter inoculated in the presence of several physicians. By 1722 the royal children had been inoculated, and interest in inoculation increased greatly. The subprefect of Mantes may well have been aware of this example. He certainly knew that Napoleon had had his son, the Roi de Rome, vaccinated in 1811, six years after the Grande Armée had been vaccinated.

[9]Officiers de santé (health officers) were medical practitioners inferior to doctors in training and with more limited privileges, who were authorized to practice by the law of 19 ventôse *an* XI (March 10, 1803).

[10] ADY, 7 M 79. A report on vaccinations in the arrondissement of Mantes between 1816 and 1854 shows 88 smallpox deaths for 1821–1830 (63 of which occurred during the epidemic years 1826 and 1827), 22 for 1831–1840, and 19 for 1841–1850.

throughout the 1820s. Madame Lainé, a midwife in Freneuse, a village adjacent to Bonnières, and one of the most successful of the vaccinators, described the problems she encountered in a letter dated May 29, 1827. Called to vaccinate in the commune of Bonnières, she found the mayor and the parish priest extremely cooperative; the priest, one Abbé Appert, announced the day and hour of her visit during mass.[11] Even so, wrote Madame Lainé, "On the appointed day . . . I vaccinated only a very small number of people. Some weren't ready, others had gone away, still other children were indisposed, with the result that I put things off." When she resumed, however, the same thing happened; and when she asked people why they were so opposed to vaccination, they "answered brazenly that they didn't want it, that neither the subprefect nor the prefect could do anything about it."[12]

Madame Lainé kept a list of those Bonnièrois who refused to be vaccinated; significantly, the seven families who gave her the most resistance conform to no recognizable pattern of wealth, education, or family size. The baker (hardly a poor man by local standards) and a café owner were as reluctant to vaccinate their children as were poor farmers and winegrowers. Vaccination seemed to them too great a novelty, and besides, it produced a series of temporary but frightening symptoms that peasants could easily mistake for the disease itself.[13]

---

[11]Appert, the parish priest of Bonnières in 1827 and 1828, stands out here as a progressive clergyman; many other preachers were less accepting of vaccination, seeing smallpox as one of the many ways in which God punished sinful man. But Appert was not only openminded; sometimes he was downright credulous. After he left Bonnières, he became involved with one Naundorff, who claimed to be Louis XVII. Appert eventually followed him to Switzerland, England, and Spain.

[12]ADY, 7 M 79.

[13]Mademoiselle Legrand, a Versailles midwife and vaccinator, described this problem in a short memoir on vaccination which she prepared in 1819 for the prefect of the department of the Seine-et-Oise (ADY, 7 M 78). Vaccination, she wrote, produced "perspiration, flabby skin, a heavy and quickened pulse . . . a change in the excretions: the urine is darker and less abundant. All these symptoms last for some time after the pimples and crusts from the vaccinations dry up and fall off." Mademoiselle Legrand stressed the importance of explaining the temporary and harmless nature of these symptoms to timorous rural populations.

During the years following the 1826 epidemic, careful records were kept on the vaccinators operating in the department of the Seine-et-Oise and on the number of vaccinations given. The vaccinators were drawn from the ranks of the usual medical personnel of the department: doctors, officiers de santé, and midwives. When the arrondissement of Mantes is considered, the midwives appear as singularly more successful in their attempts to vaccinate the local population than the more highly trained medical personnel, Madame Lainé's feelings of discouragement notwithstanding. In 1826, for example, midwives made up 25 percent of the vaccinators, yet they performed 45 percent of the vaccinations.[14] People apparently found it easier to trust midwives, familiar figures in village life, than doctors, who were separated by social class from the peasants and rarely resided in their villages. Officials at the time were aware of this phenomenon; the mayor of Gambais, for example, bolstered his argument for having the local midwife take over the vaccination program by stating that "since she lives in the commune of Gambais, she has the confidence of its residents as well as those of the neighboring towns. I think that she can have a great deal of influence on people, who unfortunately are not always in favor of vaccination."[15]

In the canton of Bonnières, also, midwives were among the most active vaccinators. The commune of Bonnières was fortunate to be serviced by two exceptionally diligent midwife-vaccinators in the troubled 1826–1827 period: Mademoiselle Damême of Limetz and Madame Lainé of Freneuse. When vaccinators were listed according to the number of vaccinations given, the names of Damême and Lainé always appeared near the top of the list. Mademoiselle Damême had even been cited for exceptional zeal by the subprefect of Mantes.[16]

[14]ADY, 7 M 79.
[15]ADY, 7 M 78.
[16]ADY, 7 M 79. After deploring the imperfect success of the vaccination program, the subprefect was heartened "to call special attention to the zeal that Demoiselle Damême has shown . . . and to her assiduity in vaccinating, especially in her own commune, almost all the people who were susceptible to smallpox. By these means, Mademoiselle Damême stopped a smallpox epidemic that was about to break out at Limetz. (Already in 1825, this midwife had vaccinated three hundred children.)"

Because of their efforts, Bonnières seems to have been spared major smallpox outbreaks in the 1820s, for the number of deaths did not soar in any of those years. As the nineteenth century continued, smallpox became less and less of a scourge for Bonnières's young; by the 1840s, juvenile mortality was down to 71 per thousand (it had been about twice that rate twenty years earlier), and it continued to decline. Vaccination was an accepted practice by the turn of the twentieth century; when the town council voted funds for compulsory vaccination and revaccination in 1905, in compliance with a national law of 1902, no objections at all were raised.[17]

Just as smallpox began to decline as a cause of death in the Bonnières area, a new and dramatic disease appeared. The reactions of the people of the Bonnières region toward Asiatic cholera shed much light on the reluctance of the peasantry to seek out medical care. The comments of the local medical personnel reveal an imperfect understanding of the disease itself, but a fairly clear appreciation of problems of sanitation and popular mentality.

Asiatic cholera made its first apearance in Europe in 1832. Originating in India and making its way westward, it was a terrifying disease, capable of killing its victims within hours. In an account to the subprefect, Dr. Dussaux, the *médecin des épidémies* of the arrondissement of Mantes and author of several perceptive reports on the medical situation in the Bonnières region, pointed to the "frightening speed with which young, vigorous men were struck down and killed within several hours" and the "discouraged and terrified state of mind of the residents of the towns where cholera had struck."[18]

Bonnières was spared cholera in 1832, although the disease

[17] Archives Municipales de Bonnières (hereafter cited as AMB), minutes of the town council meeting of November 19, 1905.

[18] Dr. Dussaux, *Rapport adressé à M. le Préfet de Seine-et-Oise sur le chólera épidémique qui a régné dans l'arrondissement de Mantes en 1832* (Mantes, 1833), quoted in Jacques Dupâquier, "Le Choléra dans le Vexin français," *Mémoires de la société d'histoire et d'archéologie de l'arrondissement de Pontoise et du Vexin* 59 (1969):72. The *médecins des épidémies* were doctors appointed by the prefects to visit and report on rural areas afflicted by disease. The institution of the médecin des épidémies has its origins in the eighteenth century.

invaded several of its contiguous villages: Bennecourt, Freneuse, Rolleboise.[19] Bonnières's escape must have been due in
no small part to sheer luck; Dr. Réaubourg, a pharmacist who
studied nineteenth-century cholera there, observed that the
town took no sanitary precautions at all when the disease
reached the Mantois in 1832. Indeed, he noted, people ridi-
culed the idea that the disease was contagious at all.[20] Scoffing
at the notion of contagion simply fitted in with the prevailing
anticontagionist theory of the time.[21] The cholera bacillus is
waterborne, and contemporary observers, while occasionally ac-
knowledging a loose connection between water and cholera,
felt that the disease came from fumes and emanations in general. By 1849, when cholera reappeared in Europe, Bonnières
was not so lucky. Fortunately, cholera did not hit Bonnières
very hard; there were only six cases and four deaths, a much
milder toll than the eighty-three cases and eighteen deaths in
the smaller neighboring village of Gommecourt, or the sixty-
five cases and thirty-one deaths at the nearby tiny town of
Moisson.

It was the manner in which cholera struck that was upsetting
for the Bonnièrois: all the deaths occurred within one family. A
belief in the contagious nature of cholera, of course, could have
easily explained this phenomenon, but not having this view, the
Bonnièrois were more inclined to see some kind of sign in the
tragedy of Tertullian Lassée, suddenly widowed and bereft of
three of his four children. The villagers were moved to an
uncharacteristic religious response. Since the deaths had occurred within a ten-day period at the end of April, the entire

[19]ADY, 7 M 49. Much contemporary interest was directed to the way in which
cholera spread. In a *Rapport sur le choléra en 1832* prepared on December 15 of
that year, the prefect of the Seine-et-Oise expressed the prevailing wisdom when
he wrote that "one constant and noteworthy fact is that the disease never spread
regularly from one commune to the neighboring commune. It burst out here
and there, like sparkles."

[20]G. Réaubourg, "L'Epidémie de choléra de 1832 dans le canton de Bonnières," *Bulletin de la société archéologique, historique, et scientifique de la région de
Bonnières* 1924, no.8:143–145. The *Bulletin* unfortunately appeared only between 1923 and 1925.

[21]For a good discussion of the strength of the anticontagionist feeling in the
nineteenth century, see Erwin H. Ackerknecht, "Anticontagionism between
1821 and 1867," *Bulletin of the History of Medicine* 22 (1948):562–593.

month of May was devoted to a series of prayers to the Virgin
for the repose of the souls of the dead Lassées.[22]

It was an interesting gesture for a village where low church
attendance had been a matter of concern for the priest for
several decades.[23] In this unexpected religious response, we
have a chance to speculate about some of the subtleties of the
peasant reaction to illness. There is little evidence to suggest
that the people of mid-nineteenth-century Bonnières saw all
disease as a direct punishment from God, but when it struck in
an especially dramatic or unusual way, or when its victim was a
particularly important person, such as the mayor of the neighboring village of Freneuse (a sudden victim of an epidemic of
"gastroenteritis" in 1830), popular reaction was one of shock
and consternation.[24] Normally, it would seem, the common
folk of Bonnières accepted illness as an inescapable part of life,
surely of the life of ordinary people.

The reluctance of the Mantois peasants to avail themselves of
medical aid supports this idea. The department of the Seine-et-
Oise had a public health service of sorts. As early as 1804,
médecins des épidémies were named in each arrondissement,
and in 1827, officiers de santé were added for each canton.[25]

[22]Maurice Poncelet, *Histoire de la ville de Bonnières-sur-Seine* (Mantes, 1947), p.
121.

[23]Abbé Dutois, in his notes on Bonnières, saw 1820 as the year when church
attendance began to decline. The earliest figures on church attendance in
Bonnières are from a pastoral visit made in 1859 by officials from the bishop's
palace in Versailles. According to this report, 100 people attended mass regularly, and between 100 and 110 people performed their Easter duty. Only 15
or 20 of these people were men. Since the population of Bonnières in 1859 was
about 750, only about 13 percent of the total population was religiously involved with the church.

[24]ADY, 7 M 56, report of Dr. Dussaux on gastroenteritis at Freneuse, 1830.
"The death of the mayor on the fourth day of an attack of gastroenteritis and
pleurisy," wrote Dr. Dussaux, "made such an impression on the villagers that
they immediately informed the subprefect." Dr. Dussaux, by calling the
mayor's ailment gastroenteritis, reveals less about his diagnostic skills than
about his adherence to the ideas of François Broussais, whose fashionable the-
ories persuaded many doctors of his day to identify many illnesses as gastroenteritis. See Edwin Ackerknecht, *Medicine at the Paris Hospital, 1794–1848* (Baltimore, 1967), p. 69.

[25]ADY, 7 M 56. The organization of this public health service is described in
a letter of February 8, 1830, from the prefect of the Seine-et-Oise to the
minister of public works and agriculture.

But in addition to dispensing medicines, the medical personnel had to wage a continual public relations campaign for their techniques. Dr. Lamayran, reporting on his problems in treating an epidemic at Dammartin in 1808, spoke of the unwillingness of the local peasants to use his remedies and of the efforts he had to make to "render medical assistance easier to use and more in keeping with the customs of the local people."[26] He leaned heavily toward the use of herb teas, which could not have differed much from local folk medicines. In 1822 the subprefect of the arrondissement of Mantes noted flatly that "one thing, unfortunately, is certain: sick people and the inhabitants of these communes generally do not trust the doctors who treat them."[27] His successor, writing a generation later during the cholera epidemic of 1849, indicated that little had changed. The toll of cholera, opined M. de Mangeot, could have been minimized had people acted more wisely; he criticized villages "where greed and avarice prevent sick people from taking time off from their work or from taking advantage of medical knowledge (which, admittedly, is often of questionable value) at a time when medical attention can still be useful."[28]

Mangeot's reservations about the ability of the medical practitioners were at least partially well taken. The doctors really had relatively little to offer in the way of effective medication and useful understanding of disease. They did, however, make a significant contribution to the fight against disease by their constant criticism of the sanitary conditions of the Mantois and their advocacy (often quite feeble, it should be noted) of better living conditions for the peasantry.

In the doctors' minds, dirt and disease were closely associated; indeed, according to them, it was evil, putrid miasmas that caused such diseases as cholera.[29] The medical personnel

[26]ADY, 7 M 56, report of Dr. Lamayran on fever at Dammartin, 1808.

[27]ADY, 7 M 56, letter of October 4, 1822, from the subprefect of Mantes to the prefect of the Seine-et-Oise.

[28]ADY, 7 M 52, letter of July 7, 1849, from the subprefect of Mantes to the prefect of the Seine-et-Oise.

[29]The miasmatic theory of disease causation is explained in Rosen, *History of Public Health*, p. 278.

of the Mantois, then, were on the lookout for fetid dung heaps, badly ventilated homes, and decaying animals, and they found them. Descriptions abound; the subprefect of Mantes, visiting the cholera-stricken town of Moisson in 1849, noted that "the greatest poverty reigns in several of the cottages I had to inspect."[30] The local *bureaux de bienfaisance* (relief committees), he added, exhausted their meager resources there within a few days. When he stopped in Bonnières on May 10 to inspect the Lassée situation, he noted that "this family lives in miserable conditions. They occupy an isolated house right near the water."[31]

The subprefect, who believed that cholera was linked to evil miasmas emanating from water, must have felt his suspicions borne out when he saw that the only cases of cholera in Bonnières occurred in a dwelling by the dangerous Seine. The modern reader, of course, is struck rather by the isolation of the Lassée house. In addition, we are led to wonder, was the Lassée household especially poor, isolated also in its extreme need? Certainly the bureau de bienfaisance of Bonnières was not exhausting *its* resources in 1849 like its counterpart in nearby Moisson, or, for that matter, at any time during the 1840s.[32] Was Bonnières in somewhat better shape from the point of view of public health and living standards than other communes in the 1830s and 1840s? Infant mortality was consistently somewhat lower in the commune of Bonnières than in

[30]ADY, 7 M 52, letter of May 25, 1849, from the subprefect of Mantes to the prefect of the Seine-et-Oise.
[31]ADY, 7 M 52, letter of May 10, 1849, from the subprefect of Mantes to the prefect of the Seine-et-Oise.
[32]Throughout the crisis of the late 1840s the bureau de bienfaisance remained solvent. Largely because of the opportunities for work in railroad construction during the 1840s and 1850s, Bonnières had few unemployed and no native beggars.

Much work remains to be done on the comparative levels of wealth of the various regions of nineteenth-century France, but when living standards in Bonnières are measured against several well-studied areas, Bonnières's relative advantage is apparent. The poverty described by Judith Lewis Herman in her study of mid-nineteenth-century Chanzeaux, for example, has no parallel in Bonnières; the province of the Nivernais, as depicted by Guy Thuillier, also appears to have suffered more greatly than Bonnières in the 1840s and 1850s. See Laurence Wylie et al., *Chanzeaux: A Village in Anjou* (Cambridge, Mass.,

other areas of rural France during the nineteenth century.[33] If conditions at Bonnières resembled those at Freneuse as reported by Dr. Dussaux in 1830, then Bonnières did have a certain comparative advantage. "From the point of view of salubrity," wrote Dr. Dussaux, "Freneuse has one of the best locations in the entire arrondissement; its inhabitants are generally strong and healthy, and do not have any endemic diseases."[34] This situation was a far cry from that of the inhabitants of the town of Dammartin. "These people," Dr. Lamay-

1966), pp. 49–52; and Guy Thuillier, *Aspects de l'économie nivernaise au XIXe siècle* (Paris, 1966), pp. 47–83.

The most interesting and precise comparison, however, is between Bonnières and the town of Mazières-en-Gâtine, a village in the department of the Deux-Sèvres which is the subject of an excellent monograph published during the Second World War. In his *1848–1914: L'Ascension d'un peuple: Mon village: Ses hommes, ses routes, son école* (Paris, 1944), Roger Thabault furnishes statistics on the number of Mazièrois who received aid from the town's bureau de bienfaisance. Since Mazières was not a particularly unusual town, it is profitable to compare these figures with Bonnières's.

During the month of December 1853, 87 people, or 9 percent of the population of Mazières, required public assistance in the form of coupons for bread or meat. In the same period, only 3 percent of the population of Bonnières, some 25 out of 744 people, were in need of similar assistance. The price of bread in both towns, it should be noted, was about the same: 1.68 francs for a four-kilogram loaf. The difference in the proportions of people requiring public assistance in the two towns was similar for the month of October 1855, another month for which Thabault furnishes statistics. Significant, too, is the fact that many Mazièrois who required aid were men; adult males represented 29 percent of the welfare population in Mazières in October 1855. During the same month, only women and children required public assistance in Bonnières.

The 1850s were not a boom period in Bonnières; indeed, as discussed in Chapter 4, they were a time of heightened emigration. Nonetheless, when Bonnières is compared quantitatively with Mazières and qualitatively with the Nivernais and Chanzeaux during those years, Bonnières appears to have been relatively favored.

[33]The infant mortality rate for the town of Boulay in the department of the Moselle, for example, was 175 deaths per thousand births for 1810–1849; it was 129 in Bonnières during the same years, a full 26 percent lower. Infant mortality figures for France generally during the same period were 186 for the years 1811–1820, 188 for 1821–1830, 175 for 1831–1840, and 159 for 1841–1850. The information on Boulay is from Jacques Houdaille, "La Population de Boulay (Moselle) avant 1850," *Population* 22, no. 2 (1967):1076. The figures for France are from the *Annuaire statistique de la France, 1966: Résumé rétrospectif*, p. 13*, published by the Institut National de la Statistique et des Études Economiques, Paris.

[34]ADY, 7 M 56, report of Dr. Dussaux on gastroenteritis at Freneuse, 1808.

ran wrote in 1808, "eat nothing but potatoes, only rarely do
they have bread; they drink bad cider or well water, they are
poorly dressed . . . , they have absolutely no firewood."[35] Freneuse, like Bonnières, was located on the Seine River; Dammartin was farther inland. At a time when economic growth
was marginal, a riverside location may have opened up just
enough auxiliary jobs to make the difference between destitu-
tion and bearable poverty.

In any event, the real improvements in diet and housing in
Bonnières did not occur before 1850. Documents from the
Second Empire point to a marked improvement in diet; during
the 1860s, a well-off farmer was consuming, among other
things, 300 grams of beef, lamb, or veal daily, and all other
agricultural personnel were eating 250 grams of pork each
day.[36] With this very satisfactory protein and caloric intake, a
noticeable increase over the diet described by Cassan in 1833,
general health and robustness were greatly improved. By the
turn of the twentieth century, the diet of the Bonnièrois had
improved even more; Louis Anquetin, the village schoolteacher, spoke of the "new needs of the working-class population, which spends much more for food and clothing than it
did in the past."[37]

Sanitary conditions in Bonnières, however, remained a serious problem. Polluted drinking water was a great carrier of
disease in rural France, and Bonnières's water supply remained
deficient until after the First World War. In 1876 the inhabitants of the hamlet of Les Guinets complained to the town

[35]ADY, 7 M 56, report of Dr. Lamayran on fever at Dammartin, 1808.
[36]AMB, agricultural survey of 1862.
[37]Louis Anquetin, "Monographie de Bonnières," p. 45. This and many of the
other communal monographs prepared by the schoolteachers of the canton of
Bonnières for the Exposition of 1900 spoke of the improved diet of the peasants. The author of the monograph on Jeufosse noted that "today's farmer has
a very strong tendency to have a substantial and varied diet and to indulge in
refined dishes" (p. 115). The author of the monograph on Freneuse noted the
progress in living standards achieved during the nineteenth century, and concluded that "it must be admitted that we are far from the time when La
Bruyère painted such a bleak picture of the country dweller" (p. 24). These
monographs may be consulted at the Departmental Archives of the Yvelines
and in the town halls of the communes concerned.

council that they needed a reservoir for drinking water. Land was bought to construct one, but it could not have been adequate, for twelve years later the inhabitants of Les Guinets brought up the issue again. It was only in the 1920s, with the construction of a new well system, that sufficient high-quality water was assured for the people of Bonnières. Good sewers were not built until the 1930s.

The story of the taming of disease in Bonnières between 1816 and 1915, then, is mixed. There were dramatic if isolated successes. The marked decline in the toll taken by smallpox is perhaps the clearest example, and the impact here seems to have been felt mainly in one discrete age group, that of children from thirteen months to four years. Other infectious diseases were much less responsive to nineteenth-century medicine and remained major causes of death in Bonnières. Infant mortality did not improve significantly until the beginning of the twentieth century, since babies remained highly subject to infections carried in contaminated milk and food.[38] Improvement in the area of infectious diseases came only at the turn of the twentieth century, as the work of Louis Pasteur and Robert Koch paved the way for a better understanding of the germ theory of disease. As the French medical establishment gave up its belief in the miasmatic theory, it could begin to deal more effectively with the problem of contagion. The story of the eradication of diphtheria, scarlet fever, tuberculosis, and typhoid, however, belongs more properly to the twentieth century.

Another medical event that appears to have been handled more effectively in the nineteenth century than in the eighteenth was childbirth. A comparison between the two centuries shows an appreciable decline in maternal deaths associated with childbirth. Specific causes of death were never indicated in the vital records, but it is striking that whereas 26 percent of all married women between the ages of 18 and 45 who died during the 1736–1815 period had had a child within the previous month, only 12 percent of similar women in the 1816–1915 period had given birth in the month before death. There are

[38]See Thomas McKeown, *Modern Rise of Population,* p. 122, and M. V. Beaver, "Population, Infant Mortality, and Milk," *Population Studies* 27 (1973):243.

several explanations for this statistic. The birth rate in Bonnières in the 1816–1915 period was considerably lower than it had been in 1736–1815, and less frequent exposure to pregnancy automatically decreased a woman's chance of a childbirth-related death.[39] The maternal deaths that did take place after childbirth (and most such deaths in Bonnières occurred in the fortnight after childbirth, not on the day of the birth) often resulted from infections such as puerperal fever. Although no useful specific knowledge about this disease was discovered in the early nineteenth century, we can point to an improvement in the routine skills and awareness of hygiene among Bonnières's midwives after 1800.[40] The late eighteenth century and the Napoleonic period had seen efforts to spread knowledge of obstetrical techniques. A poster of January 28, 1805, informed midwives in the department of the Seine-et-Oise of "a demonstration course in midwifery, for those who want to practice that branch of surgery," to be given weekly at the hospital in Versailles.[41] By the mid-nineteenth century, Bonnières midwives were equipped with diplomas from Paris, and their increased skill is reflected in the lower death rates of childbearing women.

As the nineteenth century wore on, the confidence of the

[39]The birth rate in the 1736–1815 period varied from about 35 births per thousand in the 1740s to about 27 per thousand in the early nineteenth century. By the mid-nineteenth century, the birth rate had declined to 20 births per thousand, although it rose to 24 or 25 per thousand during the 1876–1905 period because of the influx of Breton workers, who tended to have larger families (see Chapter 3). It should be noted, however, that Breton maternal mortality was not correspondingly high; the Bretons of the Third Republic presumably reaped the benefits of the midwives' skill.

[40]See McKeown, *Modern Rise of Population*, p. 106, for a discussion of possible improvements in hygiene in nineteenth-century obstetrical practice. These improvements affected home deliveries only; hospital death rates were much higher. Contemporaries were aware of this fact; McKeown (p. 105) quotes J. E. Erickson, who noted in 1874 that "a woman has a better chance of recovery after delivery in the meanest, poorest hovel than in the best conducted general hospital, furnished with every appliance that can add to her comfort, and with the best skill that a metropolis can afford."

[41]A copy of this poster can be found in ADY 7 M 78. For more details on the state of obstetrics in the early nineteenth century, see Paul Delaunay, *La Maternité de Paris: Port-Royal de Paris.—Port-Libre.—L'Hospice de la Maternité.—L'Ecole des sages-femmes et ses origines (1625–1907)* (Paris, 1909). Jean Antoine Chaptal, Napoleon's minister of the interior, founded a school for midwifery in 1802, and the Faculté de Médecine of Paris also provided training for midwives.

Bonnièrois in the medical profession apparently increased. Perhaps their trust grew as they became aware of the increased ability of midwives to deal with that most common medical occurrence, childbirth. Perhaps also, as more members of the medical profession lived in the village, they seemed less alien to the Bonnièrois than the cantonal doctors and the médecins des épidémies who visited the commune sporadically during the first third of the century. In the early part of the nineteenth century, many peasants had relied on folk remedies, bought from the grocer or procured from local healers. Pierre Louis Théodore Mouchard, for example, a grocer in Restoration Bonnières, was listed as a *praticien,* or amateur physician, when he married in 1829. Members of the Ozanne family, capitalizing on the memory of a late-seventeenth-century ancestor who gained great fame as a healer, practiced both formal medicine and healing in the Mantois in the early nineteenth century; it is safe to assume that peasants from Bonnières were among their clientele. Many local women as well as healers were familiar with plant remedies: white nettle in water to stop profuse bleeding, periwinkle in water to stimulate the milk of nursing mothers, infusion of the blue-flowered borage plant to induce sweating at the beginning of a fever, and many others. Dr. J.-N. Biraben, a physician on the staff of the Institut National d'Etudes Démographiques, has evaluated the efficacy of many of the folk medicines used in the Mantois during the nineteenth century; few of them were particularly effective.[42]

By the 1830s, however, Bonnières had its own resident medical practitioner, an officier de santé, Dr. Saucisse, who came to Bonnières as a young man from a small town in Normandy. He married the daughter of the notary at Bonnières and quickly built up a clientele, apparently from all social classes. Marie Madeleine Côté, the wife of the impoverished deaf-mute tailor of the hamlet of Les Guinets, went to him before she died in 1842, and the more middle-class innkeeper Jean Baptiste Saunier and his wife also called on Dr. Saucisse for medical attention during the 1840s. Toward the top of the social hierarchy

[42]Eugène Bougeâtre, *La Vie rurale dans le Mantois et le Vexin au XIXe siècle* (Meulan, 1971), pp. 119–132.

was Louis Victor Celles, the bailiff, and before he died in 1837, Dr. Saucisse was one of a veritable battalion of five doctors who attended to his needs.[43] A pharmacist, Guillaume Gueullette, came to Bonnières in the 1840s; although he left within ten years, and in general the turnover of pharmacists was great in nineteenth-century Bonnières, the village was never without one. When Dr. Saucisse died in 1890, two doctors were needed to replace him; that they were well loved has become a part of local legend.[44] One of them, Dr. Shussarel, was a Russian who arrived in Bonnières with his Warsaw-born wife in 1894. With Russophilia at a peak because of the Franco–Russian alliance of 1892, these representatives of a friendly country must have been greeted warmly by the people of Bonnières, especially when they produced their own Bonnières-born son in 1896.

Accidents of personality and diplomacy, however, cannot explain why Bonnières was able to support two doctors in the 1890s when eighty years earlier not even one doctor had felt it worthwhile to set himself up in practice there. Something must have happened to the mentality of the Bonnièrois during the nineteenth century to make this change possible. For the causes of this transformation, we can look to the growing attention given to education in Bonnières, the well-publicized scientific progress of the era of Koch and Pasteur, and the villagers' contact over the century with the increasingly competent midwives.

The curriculum of Bonnières's elementary schools was limited to the three Rs and religious subjects until well into the 1860s. Nonetheless, Pierre François Legrand may well have given his pupils daily admonitions on cleanliness, thus reinforcing in their minds the connections between literacy, "being modern," and staying clean. He may even have obtained a copy of Bataille's *Préceptes d'hygiène à l'usage des enfants qui fréquentent les*

[43]Notarial archives of Bonnières. These data come from the debts listed in the inventories compiled after death. People of all social classes appear to have had recourse to doctors, running up bills of from three to fifty-eight francs. What we really need to know, of course, is how doctors' fees compared with those of healers. No inventories after death listed money owed to healers. (Were people ashamed to tell the notary about them?) Eugen Weber sees no reason to suppose that healers were less expensive than doctors (*Peasants into Frenchmen: The Modernization of Rural France, 1870–1914* [Stanford, Calif., 1976] p. 153).

[44]Poncelet, *Histoire de la ville de Bonnières-sur-Seine*, p. 125.

écoles primaires, or of a similar manual. Bataille was the inspector of pharmacies for the Departmental Hygiene Council of the Seine-et-Oise during the Second Empire, and had written his manual, which the council enthusiastically endorsed, in 1849. Attention to hygiene and scientific progress may also have been a feature of the night adult education classes founded in Bonnières in the 1860s. Here motivated adults gathered to strengthen their basic skills in arithmetic and reading, and also to discuss the major news stories of the day—such as the discoveries of Pasteur and Koch. By the end of the century, people may well have had more confidence in doctors simply because they were aware of their increased knowledge.

We can see a poignant example of this heightened respect for medical skill in the behavior of the people of Lainville and Sailly, two towns about nine miles to the east of Bonnières, during an outbreak of diphtheria in 1894. In October of that year, the son of the schoolteacher at Lainville fell ill with diphtheria and died. When his daughter also contracted the disease, the distraught father appealed to a Parisian doctor vacationing in Lainville who had access to Roux's serum, and the child recovered. Word of this cure traveled quickly, and parents vied with each other to obtain the recently developed serum. Dr. Bonneau, the médecin des épidémies, reported that when a child in Sailly caught diphtheria, "her father vowed to go to Paris to find [some serum]. He was lucky enough to get some." When another child in a hamlet of Lainville contracted diphtheria, "his parents, fearing that they would not be able to get any serum, had the singular idea of transporting him to Paris,"[45] where he was admitted to the Hôpital des Enfants Malades, treated with serum, and pronounced cured. Dr. Bonneau was rightfully appalled at the prospect of sick children traveling from their villages to Paris, spreading disease on their way, and he therefore recommended that serum be made available in the provinces. What is most striking here is the eagerness of the parents to obtain medicine for their children, a far cry from the wariness with which smallpox vaccination was greeted in the early years of the nineteenth century.

[45] ADY, 7 M 57, report of Dr. Bonneau on diphtheria at Lainville, 1894.

Finally, the work of the local midwives may also have contributed to this increased popular trust in medicine. Back in the
days of the Restoration, when doctors, officiers de santé, and
midwives went around the Mantois trying to promote vaccination against smallpox, the midwives had had considerable success in convincing wary peasants that this strange new procedure was a good idea. Mademoiselle Legrand's writings especially indicate that she was sensitive to peasant fears. As the
nineteenth century progressed, the professional qualifications
of the midwives improved. A list of medical personnel working
in Bonnières during the Second Empire shows that Louise
Françoise Renoult, midwife, had received a diploma in Paris in
1841; her colleague Ludovicine Augustine Emma Saint received her Paris diploma in 1864.[46]

But while the qualifications of the midwives improved, their
social origins remained the same. The midwives were always
recruited from the local population; they were daughters of
farmers, wives of shopkeepers. Louise Renoult, for example,
had been born in the nearby town of Bréval; she entered
Bonnières with her grocer husband about the time the railroad
station was built. Ludovicine Saint, a native of the department
of the Eure, first appeared on the Bonnières census of 1866 as
the wife of Jean Pierre Palmantier, a farmer with a large extended family in Bonnières. At a time when Bonnières was
beginning to change through industrialization, the Palmantiers
were part of the old agricultural sector of the town. By marriage, then, Ludovicine Saint was associated with traditional
elements in Bonnières. The next midwife, Zélie Rouvel, con-
formed to the same pattern. Born in the neighboring village of
Bennecourt in 1860, the daughter of a roadmender, she moved
across the river to Bonnières as a child and grew up there; she
also presumably received Paris certification. Here, too, we have
a local girl of middling social origins getting herself certified
with a Paris diploma and returning to her village to practice
midwifery. It must have been easy for Bonnières women to
trust these local girls; easy too, perhaps, to listen to them when
they suggested a medical consultation for a particular ailment.

[46]AMB, ordinances of the mayor, April 1858.

But these young women were not only the transmitters of knowledge; they were also the recipients of it. With their exposure, however brief, to the subtleties of Parisian medicine, these midwives must have become much more willing to trust it themselves. And so the midwives appear as links between the stolid conservatism of their Bonnières compatriots and the esoteric and often frightening knowledge of the doctors.

This explanation must of necessity remain in the realm of conjecture. It seems reasonable to suggest that a midwife, stopped at the marketplace by a mother whose baby she had recently delivered, might respond to a question on health by referring it to the village doctor, her Paris training having taught her the necessity for recourse to more skilled authority. A midwife in a more isolated part of France or one with more rudimentary training may well have been tempted to set herself up as a competing medical authority. There is also a more down-to-earth explanation for the increased local acceptance of medical care: beginning in 1853 it became free, at least for those Bonnièrois unable to pay. From that time on, a list of people eligible for free medical care was drawn up each year; in the 1890s some forty people were on this list.[47] In 1901 a Service départemental de la Maternité was organized by the administration of the department of the Seine-et-Oise; this service, which was functioning in Bonnières by 1908, was established to provide financial assistance to needy pregnant women.[48]

This attention to the delivery of medical care to the indigent was but one manifestation of the increasing departmental and municipal concern (or at least of the increasing number of circulars) about health and hygiene from the 1880s on. A municipal hygiene commission, composed of doctors, the pharmacist, and representatives of the town council, was established in 1892. This commission dealt intelligently but with great financial circumspection with such issues as epidemics and hospitalization. In 1892, for example, a cholera-like epidemic threatened the Mantois. The Bonnières town council, doubtless fol-

[47]In 1888 the town council described this program; each indigent received about one free doctor visit a year.
[48]AMB, minutes of the town council meeting of May 30, 1908.

lowing the advice of the hygiene commission, recognized the importance of fighting disease. Nonetheless, probably for reasons of economy, it unanimously opposed the purchase, suggested by the prefect, of some complicated fumigating equipment.[49] A new hospital plan proposed the same year, however, met with the approval of the Bonnières town council, especially since it saved the commune money. According to this plan, the department was to pay 60 percent of hospitalization fees for the poor, leaving the commune's share at 40 percent. Since the commune had previously been responsible for the entire cost of hospitalization for the Bonnières poor at the Mantes hospital, the councilors obviously favored this change.[50] Medicine had become more acceptable and less mysterious to people by the beginning of the Third Republic, largely because of education, greater contact with doctors, and the midwives' work; now, as the twentieth century opened with a promise of subsidized medical care for the poor, the town of Bonnières could not afford to let this opportunity pass by.

Just as the nineteenth century saw the people of Bonnières begin to accept the ministrations of modern medicine, thereby allowing a more rational approach to the problem of disease, it also saw the weakening of the close links between the major events of human life and those of agricultural life which had been characteristic of the Old Regime. Both of these developments had implications for the demographic life of the town; both of them also reflect the stages by which the Bonnièrois ceased being peasants, chronically afraid of change, and moved into a more modern frame of mind in which encounters with new situations were approached in a more pragmatic way. It has already been shown that the acceptance of medical care produced some positive results for the Bonnièrois of the nineteenth century. The decline of farming as the mainstay of the village's economy which began during the Second Empire lessened people's dependence on the agricultural year and allowed certain sentimental changes that had probably begun in the late eighteenth and early nineteenth centuries to flourish.

[49]AMB, minutes of the town council meeting of September 14, 1892.
[50]AMB, minutes of the town council meeting of November 13, 1892.

Writing the history of human feelings, especially from demographic records, is a risky endeavor. In the world of history, Charles Tilly has wisely observed, true love leaves fewer memorials than the sale of a sow.[51] And the memorials it does leave tend to be isolated, such as the letter written in 1819 by Marie Madeleine Noel, a laundress who lived in Rolleboise, asking her father's permission to marry Jacques Aimable Saunier, an innkeeper at Bonnières. She did not write of her great love for the innkeeper, but rather noted that she had little chance of ever finding such a wealthy husband again.[52] Yet a hundred years later Bonnières was the scene of a great passionate suicide when Georgette Aguette, widow of Marcel Sembat, killed herself twelve hours after her husband's death, declaring that her place was with him.[53]

Clearly, anecdotal material alone is too isolated in nature and too dependent on individual psychological peculiarities to furnish a solid base for any sort of sentimental history. (The case of Mademoiselle Noel is surely more typical than that of Madame Sembat.) Yet anecdotes can be important, if they illustrate themes that can be corroborated by other evidence. And there are other, more statistical types of data that suggest that one of the sentimental developments of nineteenth-century Bonnières was a redefinition of the marriage relationship, with a somewhat greater emphasis placed on personal preference and love.[54]

Some of the seeds for this change were sown in the years following the Revolution, when the regular use of birth control entered the mores of most married couples in Bonnières. Although the economic advantages of contraception cannot be discounted (smaller families mean fewer mouths to feed), the use of birth control can also be construed as an assertion of the

[51]Charles Tilly, *The Vendée*, 2d ed. (New York, 1967), p. 83.

[52]Archives Notariales de Bonnières, Fonds Robert.

[53]See Albert Anne, *Cent ans d'industrie bonnièroise, 1863–1963* (Mantes, 1964), p. 14, and Louise Weiss, *Mémoires d'une Européenne* (Paris, 1968), vol. 1, p. 272.

[54]This transition is discussed in more general terms by Edward Shorter in *The Making of the Modern Family* (New York, 1975), pp. 149–150. Despite these changes, practical considerations also remained important in the choice of a marriage partner, as can be seen by the high degree of occupational endogamy in Bonnières throughout the nineteenth century.

value of sexual or romantic love in itself. For centuries birth control had been used in adulterous relations, but during the eighteenth century it was extended to married love, first among the upper classes and later among the peasantry. Ideas about the role of sexual love in marriage, therefore, must have undergone considerable change. By the end of the eighteenth century, many couples seem to have held the belief, to use Jean-Louis Flandrin's phrase, that "marriage is a love relationship legitimized as such by the sacrament."[55]

Flandrin's hypothesis is borne out in nineteenth-century Bonnières. Marriage partners were still chosen with practical considerations in mind and occupational endogamy remained high throughout the nineteenth century, but there are also indications that marriage was beginning to be viewed less exclusively as a business proposition and somewhat more as a sentimental undertaking. For one thing, as the nineteenth century progressed, men in Bonnières began taking younger wives. The average age of men at first marriage remained roughly constant in Bonnières between 1816 and 1915; it hovered around the figure of 26 years. The corresponding age for women in the same period, however, showed a downward progression. During 1816–1835, brides were fairly old; the average age of women at first marriage between 1816 and 1825 was 25.8 years, and between 1826 and 1835 it was 24.0 years. With men getting married at about 26, the result was that in about one-third of the marriages in Bonnières between 1816 and 1835, the wife was older than her husband.[56] Such an arrangement had an obvious malthusian effect, for the woman who married for the first time at age 25 or 26 had let seven or more of her childbearing years elapse. But with the widespread use of contraception, this rather indirect way of limiting family size was no longer necessary. Starting with the 1836–1845 decade, the average age of women at first marriage fell to about 21 years, and it remained at that low level until the First World

[55]Jean-Louis Flandrin, "Contraception, mariage, et relations amoureuses dans l'occident chrétien," *Annales: Economies, Sociétés, Civilisations* 24, no. 6 (1969): 1390.

[56]This phenomenon is discussed in Shorter, *Making of the Modern Family*, pp. 154–156.

War, the end point of this study. After 1865 it was the rare bride—about one in ten—who was older than her husband. "One has the impression," Marcel Lachiver wrote in his study of Meulan, and his words ring true for Bonnières, "that in the nineteenth century a wife is no longer only a fellow worker with whom one is linked up, but that she becomes more feminine, that men want her to be younger. Physical attractiveness appears more important."[57]

And when his wife died, the Bonnières widower of the mid- and late nineteenth century did not remarry as soon as his counterpart in the early years of the century. Between 1816 and 1865, every sixth widower who remarried in Bonnières did so within six months of his wife's death. In the 1866–1915 period, by contrast, no widower in Bonnières took another spouse so quickly. The explanation for the decline in precipitous remarriages probably lies in the shift away from a primarily agricultural economy which began in Bonnières during the Second Empire. To a farmer, the loss of a wife was an economic as well as a human loss. A newly widowed factory worker, small shopkeeper, or minor bureaucrat, on the other hand, could probably afford the luxury of looking around for a wife he fancied, since his occupation did not require a woman's help so strongly.

The very time of marriage, too, became more of a personal choice as the nineteenth century wore on. When the eighteenth-century calendar of marriages is considered, the marriage ceremony appears as a sort of communal rite. Clustered in the winter months of November and January (these two months accounted for almost one-third of all marriages in the 1736–1815 period in Bonnières) and occurring most often on Monday or Tuesday, weddings take on the character of a group festival, an assertion of strength against the rigors of winter. Very few weddings took place in August and September in the eighteenth century and well into the nineteenth; harvest chores presumably kept the Bonnièrois too busy for celebrations during those months. Similarly, March, which coincided with Lent, was a month with very few marriages in

[57]Lachiver, *Population de Meulan*, p. 138.

eighteenth-century Bonnières; it has already been pointed out that the revolutionary years saw a flurry of Lenten marriages, but the 1816–1865 period saw relatively few, only 2.4 percent of all marriages. By the second half of the nineteenth century, however, the earlier postrevolutionary return to the observance of Lenten prohibitions had vanished, and 6.5 percent of all weddings, almost the normal monthly average, took place in March in the 1866–1915 period.

Indeed, there are only slight variations in the monthly distribution of marriages in Bonnières in the 1866–1915 period. Couples were certainly not running to the altar (it was still the altar, even during the Third Republic) in droves in November and January. With the decline of agriculture as a major occupation in Bonnières, fewer people had to be concerned about waiting till the harvest was in before marrying. Nor did scruples about Lent prevent Bonnièrois from scheduling March marriages after 1866. From all appearances, people got married when it was convenient for them to do so. In such a trivial detail as the choice of a wedding date, we can see the quiet assertion of a sentimental individualism in Bonnières. Villagers were now making personal choices for purely private reasons. They had largely separated themselves from the matrix of demands of communal tradition, agricultural necessity, and religious prohibitions.

A similar decline in the influence of church and communal restraints on private sexual behavior is apparent when the question of illegitimacy is considered. During the eighteenth century, illegitimate births never accounted for even 1 percent of all births. In this respect, Bonnières was similar to other towns in the Ile-de-France and Normandy. The church of the Old Regime may have deplored premarital sexual activity, but judging from the considerable prenuptial conception rates all over eighteenth-century France, it was unable to convince its faithful, especially engaged couples, of the totally sinful nature of sexual relations before marriage.[58] In the matter of illegiti-

---

[58]Demographers consider a birth that occurs before the end of eight months of marriage to be the result of a prenuptial conception. Such conceptions were common in eighteenth-century France. About 10 percent of all births in

macy, however, the admonitions of the prerevolutionary church appear to have been more successful. But during the 1790s things began to change in Bonnières; the illegitimacy rate passed 1 percent for the first time during 1796–1805 and crept slowly upward through the nineteenth century. By 1856–1865 illegitimacy rates had reached 4 percent of all births, and they hovered between 4 and 5 percent until the First World War.

Although the illegitimacy rate itself did not change dramatically over the course of the nineteenth century, the circumstances surrounding illegitimacy did. Until about 1865—that is to say, in preindustrial Bonnières—the typical unwed mother was a young woman living with her parents, and the baby was her first child. Rarely did she marry the father; only four of the thirty-two illegitimate children born between 1816 and 1865 were legitimized in this way. It would appear that in the first half of the nineteenth century, an illegitimate birth did not ruin a girl's life: although some unwed mothers left the village, many stayed and later married other men. But neither was it a way of life.[59] The girl might live with her parents and child, but rare indeed was the single mother who set up housekeeping alone with her child.

The picture was quite different after 1865, when two changes in this pattern occurred. On the one hand, the number of mothers who bore more than one illegitimate child rose; nine women accounted for twenty-one, or well over a third, of the fifty-eight illegitimate births between 1866 and 1915. Many of these women lived in unconventional arrangements with their lovers. In so doing, they were openly behaving in a way that was not customary in the first part of the century. On the other hand, the parents of about a quarter of the illegitimate children born between 1866 and 1915 did get married, but

---

Bonnières between 1736 and 1785 were the result of prenuptial conceptions; this figure rose slightly in the nineteenth century. These rates are typical; the rates of prenuptial conceptions for many villages in Old Regime France are given in Jean-Louis Flandrin, *Les Amours paysannes: Amour et sexualité dans les campagnes de l'ancienne France (XVIᵉ–XIXᵉ siècles)* (Paris, 1975), pp. 178–179.

[59]Ibid., p. 231. Flandrin has interesting comments on the relative kindness with which unwed mothers were treated in rural France. They appear to have been fairly well treated in Bonnières also.

these marriages did not necessarily take place immediately after the birth. Often, in fact, the interval was considerable; the average of the fourteen known intervals is thirty-two months. The social context of illegitimate births was clearly different after 1865 from what it had been before. By the time of the Third Republic, the factories were assuming a more important role in shaping the character of the town, and migration was increasing. The rapid shift toward an industry-dominated town, the influx of newcomers, and Bonnières's increased contact with urban attitudes all helped liberalize the unwritten rules of life in the village so that some couples could feel comfortable living with several toddlers for a number of years before making their union legal.

Commercial wet-nursing was a third practice whose character was greatly modified in response to the industrial and emotional changes of the nineteenth century. During the eighteenth century, mothers in the bourg and hamlets of Bonnières, like many others throughout France, had made extra money by taking in babies to nurse. Deriving from a fear of using animal milk for babies, or from an unstated jealousy on the part of husbands loath to share their wives' breasts with their offspring, wet-nursing was a mainstay of many rural economies in the eighteenth and nineteenth centuries.[60] It flourished in Bonnières until about 1865, when it began to decline for reasons both economic and emotional.

The operation of the wet-nursing business in Bonnières was described very well by Maurice Poncelet: "The wet nurses, brought together by a recruiter, sometimes with an assistant, went to look for children in Paris; the function of the recruiter was to put these women into contact with their clientele, to drive them to Paris. . . . The trip in both directions was made in the notorious *Galiote* [a boat that operated between Rolleboise and Paris], under horrifying sanitary conditions."[61]

---

[60]George D. Sussman, "The Wet-nursing Business in Nineteenth-Century France," *French Historical Studies* 9, no. 2 (1975): 304–328. A suggestive psychological interpretation of some of the motives behind wet-nursing is given in David Hunt, *Parents and Children in History: The Psychology of Family Life in Early Modern France* (New York, 1970), pp. 106–107.

[61]Poncelet, *Histoire de la ville de Bonnières-sur-Seine*, p. 121.

Few aspects of the history of Bonnières are as depressing as the story of the city children who made this trek to Bonnières, often barely alive when they started out. If they died in Bonnières, their parents never came to the funeral, which was witnessed by the husband of the wet nurse and one other individual, doubtless cajoled into doing so by the promise of a glass of wine. The presence of the nurslings at Bonnières is perceived mainly through their death records; after 1846, some are listed on censuses.

It is difficult to know how many nurslings were serviced at Bonnières, but between 1816 and 1865, 80 percent as many nurslings died in Bonnières before their first birthday as native-born babies.[62] The situation had been similar in the eighteenth century. About three-quarters of the nurslings were born in Paris, and most of the remainder came from towns northwest of the capital city, along the route of the *Galiote*. Their parents belonged to the middle and lower classes; among them were tailors, masons, and other artisans and petty tradesmen. Suckling the children of these people provided work for at least 250 Bonnières women, mostly farmers' wives, during the 1736–1915 period. By the end of the Second Empire, however, wet-nursing as a commercial enterprise had begun to decline in the village; between 1865 and 1915, four times as many native babies as nurslings died in Bonnières, and the days when Parisian babies rivaled Bonnièrois babies in number were over.

It is not by chance that the waning of wet-nursing in Bonnières coincided with the beginning of the industrialization of the town. For one thing, as Bonnières became a settlement with factories, smokestacks, and pollution, Parisian parents must have seen little reason to send their children to Bonnières to be wet-nursed when for the same price they could send them to still bucolic towns like Jeufosse and Rolleboise. In addition, the needs of the Bonnièrois, especially the women, had changed also. Living standards had improved, and the families of the

[62]Between 1736 and 1915, 80–85 percent of the nurslings who died in Bonnières were less than one year old. It is very unlikely that their mortality rate was lower than that of native babies, and thus it appears reasonable to suggest that there were roughly four-fifths as many nurslings as native infants. The approximate nature of this calculation should be stressed.

Second Empire and Third Republic were not in such urgent need of extra cash as their counterparts of the eighteenth and early nineteenth centuries had been. Moreover, by the 1880s, factories had been established in Bonnières which were willing to hire women, and were paying them more than they could earn as wet nurses.[63] The Bonnières women who needed to work in the late nineteenth century chose to work in the factories.

The wet-nursing that did remain in Bonnières after 1866 was less purely commercial in character. In the 1816–1865 period, every sixth or seventh nursling sent to Bonnières had been the child of a young Bonnières couple that had gone to Paris to seek their fortune. After 1866, however, the proportion of these special nurslings rose to almost one in three. Not only was commercial wet-nursing on the wane with fewer nurslings entering Bonnières, but the smaller number of nurslings in Bonnières included a greatly increased proportion of familiar, loved babies. The Bonnières women of the Third Republic, it would seem, were willing to do some wet-nursing, but more and more frequently they confined this activity to babies for whom they had some sentimental attachment.

This shift takes on added significance when it is realized that during the late Second Empire and early Third Republic, the demand for wet nurses increased in the Paris basin as more Parisians were able to afford them.[64] The women of Bonnières, however, seemed reluctant to fill that role. Did they harbor feelings about childhood which made it more difficult for them to nurse other women's children for a fee? On some levels, of course, we will never know, but the nineteenth century, after all, was the time when education became widespread in Bonnières. There had been a school in the village even before the Guizot law of 1833, but school attendance was sporadic well

[63]Sussman ("The Wet-nursing Business in Nineteenth-Century France") writes that the average wage of a rural wet nurse in 1866 was 20 francs a month. During the late 1860s and 1870s, a woman worker in one of Michaux's factories could make between 1.50 and 2.50 francs a day. Since such work was always available, it stands to reason that a Bonnières woman could make more money in the factories than as a wet nurse, assuming that she worked twenty days a month.

[64]Ibid., p. 321.

into the 1850s. Agricultural needs came first, and school attendance regularly dipped in the spring, according to the figures
provided in the minutes of the town council during the Second
Empire. By the time of the Third Republic, however, attendance apparently stopped being a problem, for the references
to unsatisfactory attendance ceased. The parents of the 1870s
and 1880s seemed much more concerned about their children's
education: they sent them to schools, communal and private;
they enrolled them in youth organizations at the church.[65] The
parents themselves may have rarely set foot in church, but at
least some of them sent their children to catechism classes and
outfitted their daughters with white veils and dresses for processions in honor of the Virgin. Participation in religious activity appears to have been viewed by the parents as something
good for the children, an experience they should not miss, a
part of growing up.[66] Even musical education was not entirely
neglected in the Bonnières of the early twentieth century. Appearing for the first time on the 1906 census was a piano
teacher, unmistakable herald of the child-centered culture of
our day. Bonnières mothers of the 1900 period could not possibly have read Dr. Spock; most of them had probably never
even heard of *Emile*. But among the petty bureaucrats and
shopkeepers whose children learned to play the piano, among
the workers and farmers whose children trekked off to school
and to their after-school church activities, there obviously prevailed a mentality that put a value on childhood and perhaps
made commercial wet-nursing seem retrograde and emotion-
ally unacceptable.

Nineteenth-century Bonnières had seen a modernization of

[65]Two of these organizations were the Confrérie du Sacré Coeur de Marie
pour la Conversion des Pécheurs and the Associés du Scapulaire du Mont
Carmel. Both Breton and non-Breton Bonnièrois belonged to such organizations. I am grateful to the parish priest of Bonnières, M. l'abbé Chenut, for
letting me consult the registers of these organizations at the Bonnières rectory.

[66]André Burguière's research team, which studied the present-day commune
of Plozévet, found a remarkably similar attitude toward religious instruction.
As a local informant commented, "People send their children to catechism to
be like everyone else. All parents, even nonbelievers, have to send their children there until First Communion. Otherwise, they lose face" (Burguière, *Bretons de Plozévet* [Paris, 1975], p. 259).

attitudes on several levels. By the eve of the First World War, the Bonnièrois were able to approach the problem of health and disease more rationally and less fatalistically than had their great-grandparents. Doctors could be respected and consulted; the automatic fear that the medical profession had inspired in the past was largely gone. Emotional attitudes, too, underwent considerable transformation. At the beginning of the Restoration, the needs of the people of Bonnières were still bound up with the many requirements of church and agricultural tradition. Behavior in love and marriage, for example, had to conform to societal norms and demands; personal satisfaction was secondary to these more important considerations. By 1900, however, the matrix of external demands had lost its hold on many of the Bonnièrois. The expectations for health and satisfaction of a Bonnièrois of 1915 were probably very much like our own; those of his early-nineteenth-century ancestor, on the other hand, belonged to the proverbial world we have lost.

CHAPTER 2

The Modernization
of Agriculture

At the beginning of the Restoration, agriculture was the primary source of livelihood for the people of Bonnières. Before the coming of the railroad, half the active population of the commune devoted their days to agricultural pursuits. For such a society, the basis of wealth obviously was the land. And Bonnières was fortunate, for although its soil was not so rich as the lush fields of the Beauce, it still afforded a fairly good existence to those who lived from it.

The period 1815–1914 presented a series of challenges to Bonnières's farmers. During the Restoration, winegrowing, which had been their traditional occupation during the eighteenth century, was largely abandoned. Fields once sown in vines were, during the reigns of Louis Philippe and Napoleon III, given over to grain cultivation, especially the cultivation of wheat. As wheat prices declined toward the end of the Second Empire, however, Bonnières's farmers faced a new threat. Fortunately, by the late 1860s, efforts were being made to develop the town's agriculture and to orient it toward the needs of the Parisian market. When Bonnières and the rest of France were undergoing the agricultural slump of 1873–1896, it was precisely those sectors that had been modernized and rationalized that were able to survive. In 1892, only two hectares were sown in vines, in contrast to the widespread winegrowing of the eighteenth century. On the other hand, the large model farm set up by Jules Michaux in the 1860s was being exploited in a profitable, technically sophisticated fashion by the Société Laitière Maggi on the eve of the First World War.

Patterns of landholding varied in Bonnières during the hundred years after 1815, but one element was constant: the coexistence of a single large estate (first a noble estate and later a commercially operated farm) and a myriad of small holdings.

In the early years of the Restoration, the large estate belonged to the duchess of Berry, Marie Caroline Ferdinande Louise de Bourbon, daughter of Francis I, king of Naples, and wife of Charles Ferdinand of Artois, duke of Berry. The young duchess had a château at nearby Rosny, and her estate spread into the commune of Bonnières. Possessing 326 hectares of land in Bonnières (over two-fifths of the town's 734 hectares), she was by far the largest landowner there. Her involvement in the life of the village must have been great, although it was a remote, one-way relationship. The woodcutters of southern Bonnières—of whom there were thirteen in 1836 and whose work supported thirty-six people—leased their land from her, as did many other Bonnières farmers. She did establish a refuge for the poor on the Rosny property in 1820, but it is hard to credit the picture of her activities that emerges in the memoirs of Alfred Nettement, one of her devoted followers:

Every summer, Madame the Duchess of Berry ran to her dear Rosny, where she took great pleasure in ignoring the etiquette of the château. There she lived almost as a simple country gentlewoman, following with interest the progress of work on the estate, calling on the poor, and greeting with gracious kindness all those who came to pay their respects or to ask for aid. The mother of Henri-Dieudonné performed marvelously the honors of the domain that had belonged to the friend of Henry IV. The neighborhood was aware of her presence, and it could be said that the entire village lived from the bounty of the château.[1]

Alongside the massive estate of the duchess lay some 4,600 plots belonging to 363 owners. This extreme subdivision of nonnoble land is typical of the Seine-et-Oise, a region with a

[1]Alfred Nettement, *Mémoires historiques de S.A.R. Madame, Duchesse de Berri depuis sa naissance jusqu'à ce jour* (Paris, 1837), vol. 2 pp. 132–133.

long history of high population density.[2] Nonetheless, it is striking to observe that in 1829, the year the cadastre was drawn up, 264, or 73 percent, of the 364 people who owned land in Bonnières owned less than one hectare each.[3]

This great subdivision of land enabled most of the household heads in Restoration Bonnières to call themselves proprietors. Most of them, of course, were meager landowners, and were obliged to rent additional land to have any sort of viable farm. Jean Baptiste Moussard, for example, a winegrower in the bourg, owned sixty-nine ares and rented more from a wealthy spinster, Mademoiselle Tollay; André Grosmenil, also a winegrower, owned slightly more than Moussard, but he too had to rent land, from Jean Baptiste Saunier. Sixty-five Bonniérois had somewhat larger holdings of one or two hectares; Jean Pierre Bonnecourt, the winegrower from the bourg whom we have already met, belonged to this group, as did the Palmantier brothers, Jean Baptiste and Jean Pierre, and Antoine Zénon Chatelain, a winegrower whose family was to be prominent in the town government. François Lechasseur, a farmer in Morvent, held 5.66 hectares, and Jean Antoine Langlois, sometime schoolmaster, town clerk, and winegrower, topped the roster of resident landowners with 10 hectares.

There were two distinct categories of absentee landowner in Bonnières in 1829: small farmers and winegrowers from nearby villages who owned tiny parcels of land, and wealthier city people who owned larger plots. The twenty-six landowners from Mantes had the most sizable holdings; together, they owned 128 hectares, or about one-sixth of the commune's sur-

[2] For a discussion of the history of landholding in the Paris area, see Guy Fourquin, *Les Campagnes de la région parisienne à la fin du moyen âge, du milieu du XIIIe au début du XVIe siècle* (Paris, 1964); Marc Venard, *Bourgeois et paysans au XVIIe siècle: Recherche sur le rôle des bourgeois parisiens dans la vie agricole au sud de Paris au XVIIe siècle* (Paris, 1957); and O. Tulippe, *L'Habitat rural en Seine-et-Oise: Essai de géographie de peuplement* (Liège, 1934). Interesting comments on the high population densities of the Mantois villages that border on the Seine are found in Richard Cobb's article "Les Disettes de l'an II et de l'an III dans le district de Mantes et la vallée de la basse Seine," *Mémoires de la Fédération des sociétés historiques et archéologiques de Paris et de l'Ile-de-France* 3 (1951):227–251.

[3] The cadastre of 1829 was updated continually throughout the nineteenth century, and can be used to study land tenure in Bonnières until the First World War. One hectare is equal to 2.47 acres.

face. Among the more considerable of these Mantes-based proprietors were three widows whose husbands had been powerful
in late-eighteenth-century and early-nineteenth-century Bonnières. After the death of their husbands, they had left Bonnières for Mantes, but had not sold their land in the village.
This land, as well as the holdings of other Mantes residents,
was rented out to Bonnières farmers. Anne Michelle Germaine
Crespeaux, the widow of Robert Anselme Delavigne, for example, leased out land to Pierre Bieuville, a farmer in Bonnières; the Delavigne family had not lived there since the death
of Robert Anselme in 1814. Neither Madame Delavigne nor
any of the other widows of Bonnières notables who had moved
to Mantes around 1820 used Bonnières as a country retreat;
their holdings included vineyards, arable land, and meadows,
but not one of them contained a house.

On the farms they pieced together from their own holdings
and rented land, the Bonnières farmers of the 1830s carried out
their business. By 1836 they had virtually completed the first
major transformation in Bonnières's agriculture, the shift from
winegrowing to wheat cultivation. Winegrowing had presented
several disadvantages for the Bonnièrois of the early nineteenth
century. Bonnières's wines were mediocre in quality, and faced
competition from the tastier vintages of nearby Bennecourt and
of Argenteuil, known for their wine since the fourth century.
The mayor of Bonnières in 1822, Nicolas Poulailler, had as his
sole wine supply one *muid* (one hectoliter and forty-three liters)
of red wine from Bennecourt; as mayor, Poulailler, of all people,
should have "bought Bonnièrois." Nor was local competition the
only problem of the Bonnières winegrowers. In 1808 they were
dealt a serious blow with the completion of the Canal de l'Ourcq.
By linking the Seine and Marne rivers, the canal enabled the
vastly superior Burgundy wines to invade the Bonnières market.
By 1835, most of the wine served in Joseph Gosselin's inn was
from Burgundy; more serious, Gosselin paid about the same
prices for the wines of Burgundy and of Bonnières.[4]

[4]Archives Notariales de Bonnières, Fonds Rousselin. Gosselin had, among
other wines, 1 muid of *vin rouge du pays* valued at 40 francs and the same
amount of *vin rouge de Bourgogne* valued at 45 francs.

Bonnières farmers, especially the younger men, responded by switching from grapes to wheat. The total number of farmers and winegrowers on the censuses of 1817 and 1836 was approximately equal. But, as shown in Table 1, the balance between winegrowers and farmers shifted dramatically over the twenty-year period.

Table 1. Number and percentage of winegrowers and farmers in Bonnières, 1817 and 1836

Year	Number winegrowers	Number farmers	Percentage winegrowers	Percentage farmers
1817	54	20	73.0	27.0
1836	27	46	37.0	63.0

Source: Censuses of the commune of Bonnières.

Especially instructive is a comparison between the ages of winegrowers and farmers in the two periods. In 1817 the median age of a winegrower was 47.5 years and that of a farmer 45.4. By 1836, winegrowers were strikingly older than farmers; whereas the median age for farmers was 40.5 years, that of winegrowers was 53.7. Clearly it was the older men who were still growing grapes in 1836; young men had changed to cereal farming. The family of Jean Baptiste Palmantier illustrates the process. In 1817 Jean Baptiste was a thirty-three-year-old winegrower with four young sons and a daughter. He was still growing grapes on his two hectares in 1836, if the census designations are to be believed.[5] His four sons, however, did not follow in their father's footsteps. Two left Bonnières (an understandable course of action in a family with five children), and the two who remained, Pierre Jérémie and Victor, were regularly listed as farmers from 1836 until their deaths. By 1846 only four men in all Bonnières listed their occupation as winegrower, and by 1886 the number was down to two.

The cereal farming practiced in Bonnières was a conservative agriculture, like French agriculture generally in the first half of the nineteenth century. Armand Cassan, a close and usually

[5]Occupational designations for particular individuals on the *listes nominatives* can be checked against the occupational designations for the same people in the vital registers of the same years. In Bonnières, these designations very often match.

sympathetic observer of the Mantois peasants, loudly lamented their great reluctance to innovate, but a realistic examination of their situation during the July Monarchy makes their caution seem less unreasonable.[6] The sheer economics of land tenancy made it unwise for an individual farmer to undertake expensive modifications on rented land. Land leased to tenant farmers was let out for very short periods: three, six, nine, and only rarely eighteen years. Long-term leases were more conducive to agricultural improvement, since the tenant farmer who held his land for three or six years was less likely to make improvements whose effects might not be felt for several years than one who held his land over a longer period. Insufficient fertilizer, too, was a problem shared by the farmers of the Bonnières region and the rest of France in the first half of the nineteenth century. Low supply and high transportation costs combined to make fertilizer a scarce commodity. A report of 1848 for the canton of Bonnières pointed out that the position of the farmer was "complicated also by the difficulty of getting enough fertilizer to increase his production. The only remedy for this situation is to lower the railroad rates, which would make it easier to get fertilizer at reasonable prices."[7]

The grain-based agriculture of Bonnières in the first half of the nineteenth century, then, was vulnerable on many accounts. In the face of crop failure or poor weather, the farmers of Bonnières, like their counterparts all over France, could do

[6] Cassan was disappointed, for example, with the short life of an agricultural society founded at Mantes in 1821. Although it had one hundred members, it did not last ten years. The same experience was repeated throughout France; the agricultural societies founded during the years of constitutional monarchy failed to modify actual practice in the countryside. This question is further examined in Charles K. Warner, "The 'Journal d'Agriculture Pratique' and the Peasant Question during the July Monarchy and the Second Republic," in *From the Ancien Régime to the Popular Front: Essays in the History of Modern France in Honor of Shepard B. Clough,* ed. Charles K. Warner (New York and London, 1969), pp. 93–110, especially pp. 101–102 and 108–109. For more theoretical comments on peasant resistance to change imposed from above, see Henri Mendras, *The Vanishing Peasant: Innovation and Change in French Agriculture,* trans. Jean Lerner (Cambridge, Mass., 1970), pp. 23–24, and Marc Bloch, "Les Transformations des techniques comme problèmes de psychologie collective," *Journal de psychologie normale et pathologique* 12 (1948):104–120.

[7] Archives Municipales de Bonnières (hereafter cited as AMB), industrial and agricultural survey, September 1848.

little. Since the Bonnières grain farmers were all small opera-
tors who had to purchase additional grain to support their
families, the extremely high wheat prices that resulted from
poor conditions held no inherent advantage for them.

Their troubles began with the two successive bad harvests of
1845 and 1846. As if that were not enough, grain prices soared
again in 1854, 1855, and 1856.[8] The combined effects of these
two crises made the years between 1845 and 1856 crucial ones
in the agricultural history of Bonnières and the neighboring
towns. The problems that the farmers faced were more difficult to resolve than those their winegrowing fathers and grand-
fathers had wrestled with some fifty years earlier. Simply
changing crops hardly seemed like an acceptable solution this
time, and besides, what crop could they turn to? The gravity of
the problem becomes more apparent when we realize that
many villages in the Bonnières area (and elsewhere too) were
never able to solve it. The migration of young people from
these towns resulted in a great loss of population and vitality
during the second half of the century.

Bonnières was spared this fate because of a happy coinci-
dence of circumstances: its nonresident chatelaine felt compelled to sell her estate, and an ambitious, capable young man
began to buy it up and develop it. The association of the duchess of Berry with Bonnières was short-lived. She had bought
the Rosny property in 1818, but she had only ten years to enjoy
her domain near the Seine before the Revolution of 1830
drove her into exile with her father-in-law, Charles X, first in
England and later in Austria. While in England, perhaps fearing another revolution, she put a London banker, George
Stone, in charge of her Rosny estate. He gradually liquidated it
between 1841 and 1853, selling the bulk of it to two Parisians.
One of them held a solid bloc of eighty-six hectares and rented
it out in small plots, much as the duchess had done before him.
The other, however, sold 124 hectares to a rich and gifted
young farmer, Jules Michaux, who proceeded to exploit them
in a new and strikingly modern way until 1882.

[8]Archives Départementales des Yvelines (hereafter cited as ADY), II M 1–
14, grain prices at the market of Mantes, 1808–1894.

The residence of Jules Michaux

Jean Jules Allain Michaux was an extraordinary young man. Born in 1822 in Lommoye, a village southwest of Bonnières, he came to the town he was to transform in 1840. His father, Marin Michaux, served as Bonnières's mayor between 1840 and 1848. Before long young Jules married Rosalie Delbouve, the fifteen-year-old granddaughter of Jean Antoine Langlois, Bonnières's largest resident landowner during the Restoration. Michaux's wife was not really a country girl, however; she was born in Paris in 1826, one year after her mother left Bonnières to marry a Paris jeweler. Orphaned at the age of fifteen, Rosalie Delbouve went back to Bonnières to live with the Langlois, and soon married the enterprising Michaux. Michaux, who had a keen vision of the future, enrolled in the newly founded Ecole Nationale d'Agriculture at Grignon and went on to become a model farmer. In addition to the land he purchased in 1861 from the Berry estate, Michaux already owned 15 hectares in Bonnières; he also rented and owned some 131 hectares in the towns of Freneuse and Rolleboise, so that his farm consisted of a total of 270 hectares, 168 in arable land and 102 in woods. At the Agricultural Exposition in Versailles in 1865, Michaux's achievements as a farmer were recognized when he was awarded the prize for the best-run farm in the entire department of the Seine-et-Oise.[9]

Michaux's importance as an innovating farmer in Bonnières can hardly be overestimated. On the most obvious level, his farm stood out as a key example of land consolidation in an area of extreme land subdivision. Other Bonnières farmers did not fail to note the advantages of larger farms, and by 1911, changes that can be traced to the example of Michaux's farm could be seen in the patterns of landholding in Bonnières. Through painful consolidation and purchase, nineteen individuals in Bonnières had managed to construct for themselves landholdings of between four and twenty-four hectares; in 1829, by comparison, only four Bonnièrois owned more than three hectares. The granddaughter of Restoration winegrower Antoine Zénon Chatelain, for example, was married to a man who in 1911 owned twenty-four hectares; a descendant of the Bouviers, who had been woodcutters in Restoration Bonnières, farmed nineteen hectares of his own in the hamlet of Les Guinets. Célestine Saunier, the granddaughter of the innkeeper Jean Baptiste Saunier, married a veal merchant who owned six

[9]Michaux's professional life may have been filled with success, but his personal life contained much sadness. His only child, a son, went mad, and in May 1883 Michaux attempted suicide. He died in November 1884 and his lands were sold, mainly to a Parisian, Eugène Nicolas Guillet. The peculiar mixture of success and tragedy in Michaux's life appealed to Emile Zola, who used Michaux as the prototype for the character Margaillan in his novel *L'Oeuvre*. In the final version of the novel, Margaillan, who typifies the rich bourgeois, lives somewhat north of Bennecourt on the right bank of the Seine, but Rodolphe Walter has shown that according to a manuscript copy of *L'Oeuvre* in the Bibliothèque Nationale, Margaillan lived north of Bonnières on the left bank of the Seine, as Michaux did. Walter has also shown other similarities between Michaux and Margaillan: Margaillan's sickly daughter is Michaux's diseased son; the name of Margaillan's estate, La Richaudière, derives from Renard (from the Bonnières hamlet Mesnil Resnard, where Michaux owned much land) and Michaux. The observations of Rodolphe Walter, who has also studied the relations between Cézanne and Bonnières, are quoted in Albert Anne, *Cent ans d'industrie bonnièroise, 1863–1963* (Mantes, 1964), p. 19.

hectares in 1911, and required three hired hands to help him operate his business.

In addition to serving as a constant example of the advantages of land consolidation, Michaux introduced specific changes into the patterns of agriculture in the village, and more significantly still, accustomed its farmers to the ideas of experimentation and change. True, no other farmer possessed such vast amounts of land, but many of the transformations Michaux effected were carried out on a smaller scale by other Bonnières farmers.

Thus, when Michaux abandoned the declining practice of maintaining fallow land, other farmers followed his example, and fallow land soon disappeared from Bonnières.[10] Much of the land he had acquired from the Berry estate had been wooded; Michaux relentlessly cleared more than one hundred hectares of it and of land he owned in the communes of Rolleboise and Freneuse. Grain prices had been low between 1847 and 1851, and so the enterprising Michaux switched to cultivation of colza and sugar beets.

Colza was not destined to last long in Bonnières. It first appeared on the agricultural report of 1856, when twelve hectares of land were sown in the yellow-flowered plant whose seeds could be converted into a rich oil. Forty hectares were sown in colza in 1850 and forty-five in 1860, but these were the only years when a large amount of land was sown with the plant. In 1862 it was planted twice but yielded nothing; one further attempt was made in 1868, when three hectares of colza gave a very poor yield. It appears that after that, Michaux abandoned colza for the more dependable sugar beet.[11]

Sugar beets, which were processed into alcohol in the distillery

[10]The agricultural survey for the year 1856 (AMB) reported that there was no fallow land in Bonnières. Later reports concurred.

[11]Twenty years before Michaux undertook the cultivation of colza, Cassan had outlined the advantages and drawbacks of this crop. Although he viewed oleaginous plants such as colza as a potential source of profit for the Mantois farmer, he recognized that the farmer who wanted to raise them was caught in a double bind: he was hampered by the persistent scarcity of fertilizer and the lack of good markets, and besides, there was no place in the modified three-field system used in the Mantois for any extensive cultivation of colza. If fallow lands were sown with oleaginous plants, they would rob the soil of nutrients badly needed by the wheat crop to follow. Michaux tested colza, but soon recognized its drawbacks and turned his attention to more profitable ventures.

that Michaux constructed in Bonnières, fared very well in the village, and Michaux once again resumed his role as an educator for Bonnières farmers.[12] For, as Henri Noilhan has pointed out, "the sugar beet, enemy of mediocrity, required large doses of fertilizer and sophisticated growing techniques. . . . Because of this, the sugar beet was a veritable school for farmers and played a considerable role in the development of agricultural progress."[13] Moreover, the fertilizer used for the sugar beets helped enrich the soil, and wheat yields rose accordingly.[14]

Since the cultivation of sugar beets required fertilizer, the venturesome Michaux set up fertilizer factories alongside his distillery. The importance of chemical fertilizers had been recognized in the 1860s. When Michaux produced superphosphates through the treatment of bones, he introduced chemical fertilizers to Bonnières and saved its farmers the trouble and expense of buying them elsewhere. And Michaux's role as a teacher in the use of fertilizers did not depend on his manufacture of chemical fertilizers alone. Animal fertilizers were still used, but he substituted cow manure for the sheep and pig manure used previously, and more important, he introduced the use of animal urine as a fertilizing agent. The 1860 agricultural survey for the commune showed that 125 hectares had been treated with animal urine. The abbé Dutois in his monograph on Bonnières also noted the key importance of this step. Michaux may have had more oxen than any other farmer—he had 120 of them—but all farmers had animals whose urine could be used to fertilize the land.

[12]The annual agricultural surveys (AMB) set down 28,000 to 30,000 kilograms as typical yields for a hectare of land planted in sugar beets, but sugar beets planted in Bonnières regularly exceeded this figure. In the sixteen years for which data on yields are available, 1856–1881, the average yield of sugar beets in Bonnières was slightly over 35,000 kilograms per hectare.

[13]Henri Noilhan, *Histoire de l'agriculture à l'ère industrielle* (Paris, 1965), p. 247.

[14]Of the grains (wheat, rye, barley, and oats) regularly planted in nineteenth-century Bonnières, wheat was the only one whose yield increased between 1848 and 1915, the years for which statistics are available. Data from the annual agricultural surveys of this period show a progression from a yield of 18 hectoliters per hectare in 1846–1857 to 25.5 hectoliters per hectare in 1898–1907. The improvement was probably due to the increased use of fertilizer and also to a certain amount of experimentation with new varieties of wheat. This experimentation was first mentioned in the survey on the status and needs of agriculture of 1867. This survey, as well as the annual agricultural surveys, is located in the AMB.

Michaux was a relentless innovator—new crops, new techniques, he tried them all. But it would be incorrect to suggest that the course of Bonnières's agriculture changed completely when he appeared. For several decades after Michaux's arrival, Bonnières remained a town of polyculture where the growing of grain, especially wheat, occupied an important though not overwhelming place. The 1870s, however, brought the threat of foreign competition to wheat-producing farmers, as vast amounts of wheat from the United States, Canada, Argentina, and Russia began to arrive in Europe. The price of wheat fell precipitously: a hectoliter sold for 24 francs at Mantes in 1872; by 1885 the price was down to 17 francs.[15]

The grain farmers of Bonnières responded by growing less wheat and more oats and barley for animal consumption. Animal raising was not a completely new activity for the farmers of the Mantois, who had been raising calves for sale at Mantes and at Poissy since the eighteenth century.[16] The farmers of the early Third Republic were encouraged to raise animals not only by the declining prices of wheat but also by the promise of a great demand for meat, which was assuming a larger role in the diet of the French working classes.[17] In Bonnières, the one veal merchant on the census of 1846 had been joined by two others in 1876; beef, cattle, lambs, and pigs were also raised. The meat trade had changed since the days of the Restoration, when a farmer from Bonnières had to walk his calves to market in Mantes. Because of the improved transport possibilities offered by the railroad, calves and other animals were often sold in Paris. To help feed all these animals, much land was converted into meadows. The series of figures on meadows is incomplete, but it appears that after 1856, between 40 and 125 hectares were always planted in lucerne, sainfoin, and clover.

---

[15]ADY, II M 1–14, grain prices at the market of Mantes, 1808–1894.

[16]The veal produced in the Mantois was of a very high quality. Pihan de la Forest observed in 1788 that "the method of raising [the calves] and of feeding them makes them the most delicate in all Europe. Paris and the Court consume great quantities of them" (*Détail du Vexin français*, 1788, quoted in Jacques Dupâquier, "La Situation de l'agriculture dans le Vexin français [fin du XVIIIe siècle et début du XIXe siècle] d'après les enquêtes agricoles," in *Actes du 89e congrès national des sociétés savantes* [Lyons, 1964], vol. 1, p. 342).

[17]Noilhan, *Histoire de l'agriculture*, p. 410.

The local railroad station greatly stimulated agriculture by bringing the needs of the vast Parisian market closer to the consciousness of the Bonnières producer. Although some fruits and vegetables had appeared in the Mantes market even in Cassan's day, the existence of a means of rapid transportation to the capital gave a great boost to truck and dairy farming in Bonnières. Responding to a nationwide survey on the status and needs of agriculture in 1867, the town of Bonnières noted that the railroads had played an important role in fostering the sale of potatoes, some of which went as far as England, and of cherries and peas, which went to Rouen. The amount of land devoted to fruit cultivation rose almost 400 percent between 1829, when Bonnières had three hectares of orchards, and 1872, when eleven hectares were given over to fruit trees. Considerable quantities of cider apples were produced between 1885 and 1915. A reflection of the increase in commercial fruit production was the appearance of two wholesale fruit merchants on the census of 1906; one of them was a Parisian. Despite the railroad, however, Bonnières never became a prime supplier of vegetables to Paris, as did many towns closer to the capital, although after 1873 several small truck gardens produced for the urban market.

The railroad also gave a strong stimulus to the dairy industry in Bonnières. Although a dairy founded in 1847 lasted only a few years, later milk- and cheese-producing establishments were to become an important part of Bonnières's economy. One, founded in 1850, was furnishing three thousand liters of milk daily to Paris in 1900. A second dairy was established in 1858 by young Louis Leblond, who had come to Bonnières from the department of the Eure and married the granddaughter of Jean Jacques Maloche, a winegrower of the Restoration period. Leblond, who would eventually serve as mayor of Bonnières during the 1890s, continually upgraded his equipment and eventually employed twenty-five people in the production of butter, cream, and a variety of soft and semisoft cheeses, which he stored in cellars he owned in Puteaux before distributing them in the Paris region. Sold to Ernest Colas after Leblond's death in 1895, the dairy was still operating on the eve of the First World War.

As might be expected, Jules Michaux did not sit back idly and watch others enter the dairy business. To compete with Leblond, who was also his political rival, Michaux founded his own dairy, which eventually captured half of Leblond's clientele. A producers' cooperative, the Société Civile des Cultivateurs de La Villeneuve-en-Chevrie, was founded by local farmers in 1893. It appears to have concentrated its efforts on milk production, which increased by about one-third in Bonnières during the years following the establishment of the cooperative.

It was the Société Laitière Maggi, however, that raised commercial farming in Bonnières to a highly developed science. In 1901 this Swiss-based company began buying up Michaux's old estate. On the eve of the First World War, the Société Laitière Maggi owned some five hundred hectares in the communes of Bonnières, Freneuse, Rolleboise, and Rosny. Its activities were varied. Locally produced asparagus was dried in a factory in Freneuse for use as an ingredient in the dehydrated Maggi soup mixes. Careful cereal growing led to high wheat yields. But the area in which the Société Laitière Maggi excelled was milk production. The bacteriology necessary for good dairy farming was studied in an Institut du Lait on Maggi's Bonnières farm; scientific studies of soil composition and fertilizers were carried out there too. The superior quality of Maggi dairy products received official recognition in 1908, when the company's butter, milk, cheese, and yogurt won the grand prize at the Franco-British Exposition in London.

Agriculture in Bonnières had come a long way from the days when almost half the work force labored in vineyards that produced a frankly mediocre wine. On the eve of the First World War, only one in seven Bonnièrois was involved in agriculture; a century of emigration and small families had whittled down the numbers of farming personnel. The farming that did take place in Bonnières, however, had grown greatly in sophistication. Michaux, with his many improvements and new techniques, had set the first example during the Second Empire. The establishment of the Maggi farms in the Bonnières region marked the growing participation of the town's agriculture in the technically advanced ways of the twentieth century.

CHAPTER 3

Industrialization
and Social Change

The gradual and partial industrialization that took place in nineteenth-century Bonnières provided a sound economic base for continued dynamic village life. Without the introduction of any industry at all, Bonnières might well have gone the way of many of its neighboring towns, which experienced heavy population losses as their young people migrated to urban centers. Had Bonnières industrialized very rapidly, on the other hand, or had industry completely taken over the town, its experience with modernization might have been much more painful and divisive than it was.

The initial step in the industrialization of Bonnières, and certainly the key to the subsequent opening up and continuing development of the village, was the construction of the Paris-Rouen railroad. The establishment of a railroad station in the northeastern part of the commune in May 1843 did more than simply bring Bonnières into closer contact with Paris and Rouen. The events surrounding the building of the railroad and the opening of the station introduced the village to the problems inherent in industrialization: the elimination of old jobs, the introduction of new laboring population into the area, the pollution of the atmosphere. The reaction of the villagers to the Paris-Rouen railroad was in many ways a preview of their later reluctant acceptance of Michaux's factories and those of his successors.

Plans for a rail connection between Paris and Rouen had

been in the making since 1825.[1] But it was only in July 1840
that a contract for the actual construction was awarded to an
English company, Mackenzie and Brassey. English capital and
English workers—some ten thousand of them—poured into
France to build the railroad. Between January 1841 and May
1843, some 127 kilometers of track, numerous stations, five
bridges, and four tunnels were built. (One of these tunnels was
located in the commune of Rolleboise, just at the entrance to
Bonnières.) From the point of view of the entrepreneurs, the
construction of the Paris-Rouen railroad was a great success, as
only fifty million francs were spent.[2]

From the point of view of the people of Bonnières and of
other Seine Valley villages, however, the railroad was a total
disaster. Or at least so it seemed at the time. The immediate
threat that the railroads presented to existing transportation
jobs outweighed any rosy visions of help to commerce in the
future. Men involved in river and overland carriage transportation, innkeepers, and restaurateurs all felt their jobs threatened. For if the railroad were to transport commodities to
Rouen, Mantes, Poissy, and Paris, what would become of the
men who made their living leading the horses that dragged
barges down the Seine? And if travelers could take a train to
Mantes and Paris, what would be the fate of the numerous
carriage drivers of the region? Travel by diligence was slow and
necessitated many stops; railway trains were speedy. If the
trains replaced carriages as a means of passenger transportation, the many inns and restaurants that flourished along the
carriage routes would surely suffer.

[1] G. Subtil, "Histoire des chemins de fer dans la région mantaise," *Le Mantois*
10 (1959):10–14. The early plans for the construction of the Paris-Rouen railroad are also discussed in Georges Lefranc, "The French Railroads, 1823–
1842," *Journal of Economic and Business History* 2 (1930):311.

[2] The Paris-Rouen railroad was the first French line whose capital was obtained in part from England and which was built chiefly by English engineers
and contractors. Joseph Locke, a highly regarded English engineer, supervised
the work. Capital was raised by Charles Laffitte and the directors of the London and Southwestern Railway. The French government provided a loan of
fourteen million francs. For a more detailed discussion of the building of this
and other railway lines in France, see Arthur Louis Dunham, *The Industrial
Revolution in France, 1815–1848* (New York, 1955).

Such were the apprehensions of the people of Bonnières and the surrounding towns. The situation was not helped by the fact that the men who had the new jobs in railroad construction were strangers both to the area and to the country. And these foreigners could be a boisterous lot. There is some evidence, for example, that the English workers set up their own drinking places. Police regulations issued in September 1841 were more complete and more comprehensive than any promulgated in the previous twenty-five years. Injunctions were added against gambling and against the serving of alcoholic beverages to intoxicated people. Anyone who wished to open a café, inn, or cabaret was reminded of his obligation to register at the town hall; this directive may well have been aimed at the unauthorized English café. (The abbé Dutois was also concerned about the great number of drinking places that sprang to life when the English workers arrived; he noted the existence of no fewer than thirteen functioning cafés in Bonnières in 1845.) But drinking was not the only concern of the police: the regulations of September 1841 went on to outlaw any gatherings other than those necessary for work.

Objections to boisterous behavior, however, real as they surely were, paled in comparison with the deep-seated hostility felt by the many people who feared that the railroad would eliminate their means of livelihood. Local antagonisms mounted, and troops had to be sent to Bonnières, Freneuse, and Rolleboise to ensure the safety of the railroad workers.[3] Finally, during the Revolution of 1848, violence broke out, and an angry band in Rolleboise burned the tunnel there. Destruction of railroad equipment was a common occurrence in the Paris region during the Revolution of 1848, but the burning of the Rolleboise tunnel during the night of February 23–24 was one of the earliest episodes. Several days later, after the revolution was clearly under way, damage was also inflicted on railroad property at Saint-Denis, Asnières, Colombes, Mantes, Meulan, and Pontoise.[4] An

[3]Cyril Richomme, "Monographie de Rolleboise" (1899), p.48, in the Archives Départementales des Yvelines, hereafter cited as ADY.

[4]The dates for these riots are from Donald W. Mitchell, "The French Railroad Attacks: February and March 1848," senior honors thesis in history, Harvard College, 1968.

The entrance to the railroad tunnel

eyewitness account of the tunnel burning is reproduced in the
Rolleboise communal monograph of 1900; it is well worth quot-
ing in part, because we find here many of the elements of the
"righteous mob"—a group of people who obey certain rules
even in the midst of their destructiveness and who are treated
courteously by the local authorities.

On February 23, 1848, during the revolution, a group of innkeepers,
boatbuilders, stableboys, and women . . . decided in the darkness . . .
to burn the railroad watchman's shelter and then to tear up the rails
and destroy the track. During the night of February 23–24 they carried out their plan. . . . After seizing the light in the watchman's
shelter, they crossed the tunnel singing the "Marseillaise." [On the
other side of the tunnel was the queen's personal railway car.] The
Rolleboise insurgents probably knew it was there . . . the women entered the royal coach dancing and singing, "I am the queen! I am the

queen!" They wanted to make off with baubles and colored clothes from the coach. The head of the band said, "We are here to burn, not to steal." After these words, the whole group set fire to the coach, which in turn spread the fire to the entire tunnel.

All the neighboring communes were in turmoil, and the National Guard of Bonnières, Bennecourt, and Freneuse were armed and stationed on the railroad bridge, but thinking that a veritable army of insurgents from Paris or Rouen was at work, they did not dare advance. When the National Guard learned that all that pillage was the work of a handful of people from Rolleboise, they approached the fire, but it was impossible to save anything.

The insurgents left the scene of the crime and went off to eat in a neighboring inn, without having been troubled by the National Guard.[5]

In this Luddite-style episode, destruction of the offending tunnel and tracks was the sole aim. No other mischief was tolerated by the head of the band of insurgents; the Rolleboise women who coveted the queen's lovely trinkets were forced to put them back into the fire. A parallel can be seen between this episode and the actions of crowds in the same region in 1775 and 1795, when enraged and hungry mobs called for the *taxation du pain* (the forced selling of bread at a price that seemed fair to them), but forbade its outright theft.[6] Interesting, too, was the action of the National Guard. The eyewitness account indicates that the guardsmen tried to stop the fire from spreading but made no attempt to punish or shoot at the offenders. But who, after all, composed the National Guard of Bonnières, Bennecourt, and Freneuse if not the brothers and uncles of the very men who would be put out of work by the railroad? Arrests were made the following day, and the offenders were

[5]This account is taken from the communal monograph of Rolleboise, pp. 48–50 (ADY).

[6]See George Rudé, *The Crowd in History: A Study in Popular Disturbances in France and England, 1730–1848* (New York, 1964), especially chaps. 1 and 7 and Part II, for a general analysis of the behavior of such mobs. Richard C. Cobb, "Les Disettes de l'an II et de l'an III dans le district de Mantes et la vallée de la Basse Seine," *Mémoires de la Fédération des sociétés historiques et archéologiques de Paris et de l'Ile-de-France* (1951):227–251, discusses similar riots that occurred in the Mantois in 1775 and 1795.

tried in Mantes and received lenient sentences, except for the
leader, who was given five years in prison.[7]

The villagers eventually made their peace with the railroad,
although for several years the Bonnières town council was em-
broiled in a dispute with the railroad company over compensation for land used by the company. For the remainder of the
century, between ten and sixteen people, usually recruited from
the local population, were employed by the railroad. François
Crot, for example, who had run a restaurant in prerailroad
Bonnières, worked for the railroad company, according to the
censuses of 1846 and 1856. Not all the stories of Bonnièrois put
out of work by the coming of rail transit, however, have such
satisfactory endings. Joseph Gosselin, the innkeeper, had died in
1833 and his widow and her new husband kept up the inn as
long as they could, but by 1846 her second husband was a day
laborer and the couple left the commune in the decade of hard
times, the years between 1846 and 1856. But despite the initial
job displacement and grief that the railroad caused the people of
the Bonnières area in the 1840s, it was to make great contributions to the prosperity of the region as the century wore on. For
the railroad did more than bring a new means of transportation.
The presence of a railway station in the village led to great
changes in the social composition of the town. Stratifications that
had not previously existed were now introduced into the fabric
of village society. At the beginning of the Restoration, Bonnières
society had been, for the most part, remarkably homogeneous.
It was composed of a broad base of agriculturalists supplemented by a very thin layer of notables, remnants of the Feugère
and Delavigne families whose heyday had been in the eighteenth
century. The Feugère family had held the lucrative and presti-
gious monopoly of the post relay, and had even produced a
minor political figure, Jean Jacques François Feugère, *avocat au
Parlement, bailli* of La Roche Guyon and Bonnières, and deputy
to the National Assembly during the Revolution. The Dela-
vignes had held important positions as officials of the royal for-

[7]Maurice Poncelet, *Histoire de la ville de Bonnières-sur-Seine*, (Mantes, 1947),
p. 77.

ests at Bennecourt. By 1830, however, the influence of these families had waned in Bonnières: the men had died leaving no sons; their widows had moved to Mantes. The fading out of the old notable class is responsible for the absence of tension when the new notables, attracted by the railroad, settled in Bonnières in the 1840s.

Beneath this thin layer of rapidly disappearing notables were the remainder of the Bonnièrois. Distinctions of wealth and cultural level do not appear to have been enormous among them. The electoral list drawn up in 1837 showed only one town resident who paid more than two hundred francs in taxes: Jean Antoine Langlois, the village's largest native landholder and the grandfather of Jules Michaux's future wife. Three other villagers paid between one and two hundred francs; everybody else fell under the hundred-franc line.

Within the great mass of Bonnièrois, of course, differentiation did exist, and nowhere is it clearer than in the choice of marriage partners. Not only did village marriages unite families of roughly similar incomes, they often followed specific occupational lines very closely. Thus both Baptiste Zénon Chatelain and Sophie Hyacinthe Daumet, who married in 1831, came from winegrowing families, and their means must have been similar, for the groom's father's tax of forty-four francs was not too widely separated from the thirty-seven francs paid by the bride's father. To be sure, when another Chatelain, François Martin, married Marie Catherine Chaptois in 1818, the difference in tax assessment was greater: François Martin, a *sous-lieutenant,* paid fifty-two francs, whereas the bride's father, a winegrower, paid only thirty-five. But in this case, the ages of the spouses may have been a factor, for François Martin Chatelain was thirty-five years old at the time of his marriage and his bride was only twenty. Extreme but not atypical cases of endogamy in artisanal groups are seen in the 1818 marriage of the mason Louis Honoré Ferrand, whose father, brother, and father-in-law were also masons, and the 1836 marriage of the ropemaker Pierre Thomas Lemoine, whose father was also a ropemaker, as were the father and a cousin of the bride.

The coming of the railroad changed the tenor of village life greatly. It would be naive to suggest that a ready-made middle class stepped off the first train that entered Bonnières, but the early 1840s did see the rapid growth of a new class whose wealth was in commerce and in professional skills, not in land. From 1836 to 1846, the number of people belonging to the commercial and upper classes virtually doubled.[8] These men brought wealth to the town; in 1837, as we have seen, only four resident electors had paid more than one hundred francs in taxes, but by 1846 this figure had grown to twelve.[9] The importance of these ten years as a watershed in the formation of a commercial–upper-class sector in the town can be appreciated when the proportions of people involved in six sectors of the economy are compared for the census years from 1817 to 1906. These data are presented in Table 2.

As clear as the increase in the importance of the commercial–upper-class sector between 1836 and 1846 is the decline in the importance of agriculture as an economic activity in Bonnières. These two trends are related; the villagers of 1817 and 1836 lived rather closely from the products of their agriculture, for only two grocers were needed to satisfy the wants of the town. But by 1846, tastes had become more sophisticated and desires more varied. Six grocers were able to stay in business catering to the expanded alimentary needs of the town, which now boasted a pastry shop, a pork store, and three wine merchants as well.

The 1840s, then, witnessed a spurt in the growth and diversification of commerce in Bonnières. They also saw a great influx of people who would eventually become political leaders there. Fully one-third of the men who entered Bonnières with their families between 1836 and 1846 and remained there for at least ten years were to serve on the town council, and two

----

[8]In 1836 fifteen men were involved in commerce and eighteen belonged to the upper classes—that is, they were government bureaucrats, doctors, teachers, and *rentiers*. By 1846, twenty-one men were employed in commercial jobs and thirty-nine belonged to the upper classes.

[9]Archives Municipales de Bonnières (hereafter cited as AMB), electoral lists of 1837 and 1846.

Table 2. Percentage of the work force in six sectors of the Bonnières economy, 1817–1906

Year	Size of sample	Agricultural	Artisanal	Transportation and hotels	Industry	Other[a]	Commercial and upper class
1817	193	50.3	13.5	16.6		6.6	13.0
1836	263	49.4	16.0	8.7		13.3	12.6
1846	268	39.9	16.8	9.7		11.2	22.4
1856	235	44.3	11.0	9.4	1.3	8.9	25.1
1866	323	30.1	16.4	5.0	14.5	11.4	22.6
1876	346	22.8	13.0	3.5	25.7	10.1	24.9
1886	384	18.5	17.5	5.2	23.4	10.4	25.0
1896	458	13.3	18.1	4.4	26.8	12.9	24.5
1906	438	14.1	15.7	8.4	24.4	12.8	24.6

Source: Censuses of the commune of Bonnières, 1817–1906.

[a]Includes the increasingly important category of household servants.

served as mayor. In terms of the commercial and administrative life of the village, the early 1840s were indeed a time of great renewal.

Just as the village had recovered from the birth pangs of the railroad, a new entrepreneur appeared in Bonnières. When Jules Michaux set up his model farm, he also proposed to process the crops he grew. To this end he created a distillery at the eastern end of the village to transform his sugar beets into alcohol. The distillery, which stood on the site of Jean Antoine Langlois's old house, was the first of a series of agriculturally based industries that Michaux was to establish between 1851 and 1882. Michaux also laid the foundations of the chemical industry in Bonnières; this aspect of his career will be analyzed separately, after his agricultural industries are considered.[10]

Michaux enlarged the distillery in 1855 and added new steam equipment in 1857 and 1859. Sugar beets were by no means the only commodity that Michaux processed; his distillery also converted barley, rye, corn, rice, buckwheat, apples, and potatoes into alcohol. In 1860 the distillery produced six thousand hectoliters of alcohol from these raw materials. Some fifty men and thirty-two women worked there from October to May (Michaux did not employ children); during the summer months these day laborers doubtless performed agricultural tasks on Michaux's farm. Many of his workers lived in outbuildings on his property; the 1856 census lists ten workers who lived with the Michaux family, and the 1866 census lists nineteen. Housing conditions for these workers, many of whom were Breton, were at best barely adequate; Albert Anne dryly observes that "on the Michaux estate, the Breton workers slept more or less everywhere— everywhere, that is, except in a bed."[11]

The distillery, Michaux's first industrial venture, received a somewhat warmer acceptance from the villagers than the railroad. Here was an establishment that provided some employ-

[10]The following pages draw heavily on Albert Anne, *Cent ans d'industrie bonnièroise, 1863–1963* (Mantes, 1964).
[11]Ibid., p. 129.

ment and did not smell too bad. When, for example, a problem arose concerning liquid waste disposal from Michaux's distillery, all parties tried to find an amicable solution. The mayor wrote to the prefect in February 1859 that "we want . . . to show the goodwill we feel in regard to the factories that are bringing affluence to our workers."[12] Michaux eventually agreed to finance a small sewer. Nor did Michaux's attempt to establish a pigsty meet with any opposition. No complaints were filed at the public hearing, and so in the fall of 1859 Michaux was authorized to run two small pigsties in the village. A paramount consideration in the granting of this approval was the fact that no houses were contiguous to the pigsties—none, that is, except two small ones inhabited by workers at the pigsty.

Michaux also received authorization in 1867 to establish a sugar refinery for his beets, but it is unclear whether it ever actually functioned. In any event, this was the last of his projects to go unprotested by the populace. In July 1869 Michaux began to produce glue in the middle of Bonnières, and his public relations troubles began.

Michaux had already established a glue factory in nearby Freneuse, so the people of Bonnières knew what they were up against—the smells of putrifying animal carcasses, noxious miasmas filling the air. Michaux, anticipating trouble, tried to pass off his Bonnières glue factory as an establishment for the production of gelatin. But nobody was fooled. In August 1869, only a month after Michaux had begun producing glue in the middle of Bonnières, the town council issued an unusually forceful protest; among its complaints were the following practical considerations:

[The factory] is situated on the main street of the town. . . . [It is surrounded by] numerous homes and large commercial enterprises, notably hotels for travelers which form the bulk of the wealth of their owners. . . . If gelatin by itself has no unpleasant or unhealthful odors, the same cannot be said of the raw materials that would be brought to the factory, which are mainly the remains of animals that have been dead for a fairly long time. . . . The by-products of gelatin manufac-

[12]AMB, letter from the mayor of Bonnières to the prefect of the Seine-et-Oise, quoted in the minutes of the April 25, 1859, meeting of the town council.

ture would decompose and putrify immediately, and cause dreadful
odors that would be harmful to public health.[13]

Michaux was also charged with being a willfully selfish person whose devotion to his own material gain excluded respect
for other people's property rights. The town council stated
flatly that had he cared one whit about the quality of public
health, he easily could have located his factory farther away
from the core of the village. This was a constant theme of the
protests directed against Michaux. The employment opportunities that his enterprises brought to the village were so great
that no one actually wanted him to leave; all they wanted was
that he locate his more foul-smelling projects at a reasonable
distance from heavily populated areas. The mayor echoed
these feelings and added that all citizens had the right to
breathe pure country air.

Indeed, Michaux seems to have cared little about the quality
of the environment. Complaints had been registered about his
habit of driving open wagons filled with fetid liquid manure
down the main street of the village. A town ordinance had to
be issued restricting the hours and streets that could be given
over to this noxious transport.

As the years passed and the "gelatin" factory stayed in the
middle of town, public annoyance mounted. A petition with
which the mayor associated himself was circulated in 1873, asking that Michaux's glue-making operations be restricted to his
other factory in Freneuse. (The Freneuse factory, which also
produced fertilizer, was located in an empty field more than a
kilometer from the nearest dwelling.) Sixty-five people signed
this petition, which was turned down in 1874. Michaux mean-
while bought more and more equipment, added soap to his
repertory of manufactured goods, and continued to foul the
air of the village.

Even after Michaux's death in 1884, the complaints about the
pestilential factories continued. Louis Gentil had bought the
Bonnières distillery, as well as the glue factories in Bonnières
and Freneuse, from Michaux in early 1884. Gentil continued to

[13]AMB, minutes of the town council meeting of August 16, 1869.

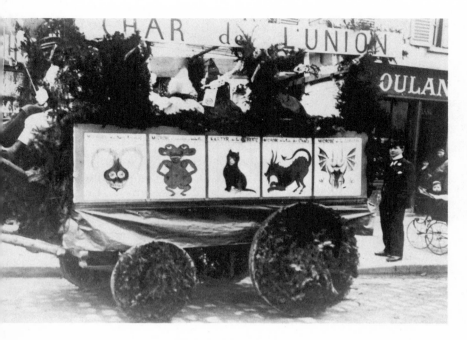

A protest against the Gentil factories

run them, but he provided employment for fewer Bonnièrois
than had Michaux. Whereas Michaux had given work on a
regular basis to some 140 villagers in his factories and on his
large model farm, Gentil, who did not exploit the farm, provided work for only 50 people.[14]

Gentil had not been running the factories for five years before
public murmurings began again about the noxious vapors they
emitted. A local health officer attributed the high incidence of
conjunctivitis in Bonnières to the presence of putrid matter in
the air; this view, however, was not supported by the Conseil
d'Hygiène of Mantes.[15] Unpopular, too, was Gentil's habit of

[14]In his "Monographie de Bonnières" (ADY), Louis Anquetin noted that
when Gentil ran the distillery, fifty people worked in it for 180 days a year.
After Michaux's death, his large farm was split and sold to several buyers.
Between 1909 and 1914, the Société des Boissons Hygiéniques, later known as
the Société Laitière Maggi, began buying up Michaux's old farm at Bonnières.
The operation of this farm is described in Chapter 2.

[15]Anne, *Cent ans d'industrie bonnièroise,* p. 117.

transporting animal bones with decaying flesh still clinging to them in open wagons along the town's main streets. Protests continued; the mayor, draped in his tricolored republican cummerbund, tried to stop a carter from proceeding with the dread cargo; and finally a mayoral ordinance directed Gentil to transport the offending bones in hermetically sealed vans.[16]

The distilling of sugar beets and the making of glue from animal bones were industries closely tied to an agricultural community for their raw materials. The chemical industry that Michaux pioneered in Bonnières, however, was less directly linked to agricultural exploitation.

The reasons that prompted Jules Michaux, a highly trained agronomist, to open a petroleum refinery in 1863 in Bonnières remain unclear. But he went into the petroleum business with his usual thoroughness and verve, borrowing large sums of money from the Comptoir d'Agriculture and the Crédit Agricole in 1864 and 1867. Yet Michaux realized that his real skills lay elsewhere, and he sold his petroleum refinery in 1869 to the Société Gérard, the first of a series of Belgian companies that would run the refinery. Most of the technically trained personnel were Belgian, but according to the census of 1872, thirty Bonnièrois were employed at the refinery.

Sold again in 1877, the petroleum refinery became the property of the newly formed Société Anonyme de Lille et Bonnières, so named because its operations included a similar factory at Lille. By 1899 some ninety workers were employed in the Bonnières factory, which produced gasoline, petroleum jelly, paint, motor oil, superphosphate-based insecticides, and fertilizers.

Fertilizer production was a logical accompaniment to the refining of petroleum; the sulfuric acid that had been used in the refinery for the rectification of petroleum could be used to turn natural phosphates into fertilizer. Fertilizer production, however, had never been popular with the people of Bonnières, and once again outcries arose over the unhealthful character of the operation.

[16]AMB, ordinance of the mayor, July 15, 1902. The town gendarmes were instructed to see to the execution of this order.

The petroleum refinery

Le Camphre factory

Since the Lille-Bonnières plants were not located right in the center of the village, but rather at its west end, complaints could not capitalize on its location, as in the case of Michaux's midtown glue factory. The town had learned by its experience with Michaux and Gentil that vigorous protests and chidings about the concern a citizen should have for the health of his compatriots rarely produced results; consequently, when the same odor problem arose from the Lille-Bonnières fertilizer factory, the town council resorted to direct injunctions against fertilizer production. The directors of Lille-Bonnières always found ways to circumvent them, but finally, tired of constant wrangling with the local authorities, they sold their Bonnières plant in 1907. The new owner, a Paris-based company called Le Camphre, produced artificial camphor and various hydrocarbons in the factories at the west end of town.

Predictably, the presence of these factories greatly altered the balance of social classes in Bonnières. At the beginning of the Third Republic, large numbers of young workers came to staff Michaux's factories and to work on his farm. By 1876, in fact, about 25 percent of the work force was involved in industrial occupations, and this figure was maintained thereafter. Who were these workers and what did they want?

Many, perhaps most, of the workers in Michaux's factories were of Breton origin, young men and some young women from the department of the Côtes-du-Nord. Underdevelopment and lack of employment opportunities were chronic problems in Brittany, especially in the inland sections. These areas were very densely populated, with some forty to sixty persons per square kilometer in the second half of the nineteenth century; the corresponding figure for the rest of rural France varied between twenty and thirty.[17] When the railroads penetrated these heavily populated communes after 1850, a great current of emigration began. Most Bretons who left went toward Paris and the rich countryside of the Seine-et-Oise, although large contingents went to the Seine-Inférieure and the

[17]Philippe Ariès, *Histoire des populations françaises et de leurs attitudes devant la vie depuis le XVIIIᵉ siècle* (Paris, 1948), p. 19.

Maine-et-Loire as well.[18] Bonnières was but one of many towns in the Seine Valley to receive poor young migrants from Brittany, and most of them were from one fairly well-defined region of the Côtes-du-Nord. Breton emigrants did not search out cheap farms to rent, but preferred to work as laborers. Michaux's large farm and factories, therefore, attracted many migrants from the Côtes-du-Nord.

Once arrived in Bonnières, the Bretons did not form an alienated, depressed proletariat, or if they perceived themselves as such, they did very little to let others know about it. By making few demands on the other villagers, they blended into Bonnières society. Residentially and socially, the Bretons were by and large segregated. They often lived together, young men huddled in worker dormitories, young couples in houses with additional young Breton workers as lodgers. Such arrangements, of course, led to severe overcrowding. At the beginning of 1851 the town council had deemed it unnecessary to appoint a commission to investigate marginal housing, but in the fall of 1864, when the village's industrial activities had been in progress for only a few years, a committee composed of a doctor, a mason, and three town councilors was formed to check on rented houses. Problems with overcrowding persisted, however; their causes were enumerated in a report of 1882:

Several lodgings occupied mainly by workers present all the characteristics of insalubrity. Indeed, rented at first by a reasonable number of workers, these lodgings, through successive sublets, end up harboring a much greater number of people than their floor space and construction allow. As a result of this overcrowding, these lodgings become unhealthful. To let such a state of affairs continue would be to neglect the health of the inhabitants and to expose the town to epidemic diseases.[19]

Another commission was named, but it, too, produced few results, for when model sanitary rules were circulated for rural communes in 1906, the town council's response was sarcastic at best. After noting that most of the stipulations did not apply to

[18]Jean Choleau, *L'Expansion bretonne au XXe siècle* (Paris, 1922), p. 78.
[19]AMB, minutes of the town council meeting of July 4, 1882.

Bonnières, the council asserted that it "approved of the rules in theory but could not approve them in fact [because] if these rules were to be implemented in Bonnières, half the buildings in the town would have to be destroyed."[20]

Bretons, then, simply remained in the substandard housing. Since the employment opportunities open to them in Bonnières were vastly superior to those in their villages of the Côtes-du-Nord, they did not complain. And since they did not take away jobs from native villagers or try to penetrate their family life, the richer or more permanent residents of the town did not complain either.

For marriages between Breton workers and girls from outside the Côtes-du-Nord were rare. Strictly speaking, as far as income and prospects were concerned, there was little reason why a Breton distillery worker should not have married the daughter of a postman or a middling farmer in Bonnières. And in fact, several of these unions did take place; between 1858 and 1874, the six young men from the Côtes-du-Nord who got married in Bonnières chose brides who had been born in the village or whose families had been established there for some time. After 1874, however, this pattern of frequent inter-marriage was reversed. It was at this point, it should be noted, that Bretons began coming to Bonnières in great numbers (some 25 percent of the immigrants to Bonnières between 1876 and 1886 had been born in the Côtes-du-Nord). Their group identity and their unpopular traits—minor as they were—were surely perceived most strongly at this time by the native towns-people. In 1882, for example, the abbé Poiffait observed that "only the grossest vices are noticed among them: drunkenness and its consequences, in women as well as in men."[21] At such a point, perhaps, the other villagers were not so eager to see their daughters marry Bretons. In any event, after 1877, rare indeed was the marriage involving a Breton in which the other partner too was not from the Côtes-du-Nord. During 1877–

---

[20]AMB, minutes of the town council meeting of February 4, 1906.

[21]ADY, II V 29. The abbé Poiffait was the parish priest of Bonnières between 1876 and 1881, and in that capacity prepared a report on the parish in connection with the pastoral visit of 1879.

1915, forty-six marriages involving Bretons were celebrated in Bonnières; in thirty-six of them, both partners had their origins in the Côtes-du-Nord.

Bretons differed from other villagers in other ways also. A handful of Breton couples lived together without benefit of clergy, although in all fairness it must be observed that such behavior was not totally new in the village. Back in the 1860s, the abbé Dutois had complained of an unwed couple living together in one of the hamlets. The Bretons had more children than the other Bonnièrois, and these children had a higher infant mortality rate than those born to non-Breton Bonnièrois.[22] There is even evidence that suggests that adult Bretons died earlier than people born in Bonnières.[23] Bretons spoke their own language, and were much less literate in French than the other residents of Bonnières. This trait was especially pronounced among the earlier Breton immigrants to the village; of the twenty Breton men whose marriages were celebrated in Bonnières between 1856 and 1885, eleven, or 55 percent, were unable to sign their names.[24] The corresponding figure for illiteracy among the

[22]The census of 1876 listed 91 people in Bonnières who had obviously Breton surnames or were otherwise known to be of Breton origin. They represented 9.8 percent of the town's population of 929. During the ten years surrounding the 1876 census (1871–1880), however, Breton families accounted for 13.1 percent of all births in Bonnières. This disparity is even greater in the later nineteenth century. By the same calculations, Bretons accounted for 10.2 percent, 7.1 percent, and 7.5 percent of the population of Bonnières in the years 1886, 1896, and 1906 respectively, but Breton births in the ten-year periods surrounding each of these censuses accounted for 18.7 percent, 13.9 percent, and 15.9 percent of all births.

The poorer survival rate of Breton infants born in Bonnières is apparent when infant mortality is calculated for 1876–1885 and 1886–1895, first with and then without the Breton births. In 1876–1885 the mortality rate for all Bonnières babies was 164 deaths per thousand births, but when Breton infants are omitted from the calculation, it falls to 132. Similarly, in 1886–1895 the mortality rate for all Bonnières babies was 140; for non-Breton babies only, however, it was 105.

[23]The average age at death of adult Bretons (over twenty years) in Bonnières is consistently much lower than the average age of non-Breton adults in the community. This disparity is partly due to poorer health conditions among the Bretons, but the generally lower age of the Breton population in Bonnières is an important factor too.

[24]See Eugen Weber, *Peasants into Frenchmen: The Modernization of Rural France, 1870–1914* (Stanford, Calif., 1976), p. 320, for a discussion of school attendance in the Côtes-du-Nord.

185 other bridegrooms in this period was 6.7 percent. Although literacy rose among the Bretons after 1885, it still remained lower than for the population at large.

There seems to be little doubt that the Bretons were a comparatively disadvantaged segment of the population in Bonnières. Yet they never "caused trouble," and seemed to have accepted the power situation for what it was. There was, for example, no worker movement at the Bonnières factories comparable to the agitation at the glassworks of Carmaux at the beginning of the twentieth century.[25] A company union had been formed in one of Gentil's factories; yet there were no strikes, no efforts to make the union a militant organization. Breton feelings of frustration, and it is hard to believe that there were none, remained pent up and controlled; indeed, it can be suggested that whatever rough consensus prevailed on basic social and personal values was able to exist precisely because of the constant repression, the everlasting refusal to complain on the part of the Bretons.

Why, we might well ask, should people behave this way? The most important reason for the docility of the Bretons was the steady employment so easily available in the town. The Bretons had come looking for work; having found it in the factories, they feared any agitation that might make them lose it. Wages in Bonnières were not bad; at the Lille-Bonnières factories at the turn of the twentieth century, they ranged between 3.25 and 7 francs for a ten-hour day. In Gentil's factories, wages were between 3 and 4 francs a day for men, 1.50 and 2.50 francs for the women and children glue workers.[26] Wages in the Côtes-du-Nord were much lower; a male farm worker made only 143 francs a year, according to the decennial survey of 1882.[27] Not only were the wages in Bonnières attractive; the work was regular. There was only one period, in the early 1880s, when minor restructuring in the factories led to some layoffs. Predictably, immigration to Bonnières temporarily declined, but by 1886, when the factories were operating at full

[25]For a study of a very different worker population, see Joan W. Scott, *The Glassworkers of Carmaux: French Craftsmen and Political Action in a Nineteenth-Century City* (Cambridge, Mass., 1974), especially pp. 139–166.
[26]Anquetin, "Monographie de Bonnières," p. 63.
[27]Quoted in Elie Gautier, *Un Siècle d'indigence: Pourquoi les Bretons s'en vont* (Paris, 1950), p. 105.

speed once more, immigration picked up and unemployment was never a problem again. For a Breton worker, unsure of finding any work at all in the overcrowded, underdeveloped Côtes-du-Nord, the promise of steady employment in Bonnières was a real attraction.

Other factors, too, help explain the stability and lack of rebelliousness among the Bretons in Bonnières. The vast majority of those whose birthplaces can be identified came from a fairly well-defined area in the department of the Côtes-du-Nord made up of parts of the arrondissements of Saint-Brieuc, Guingamp, and Loudéac.[28] The small towns of Canihuel and Le Bodéo, for example, sent more than eleven emigrants each to Bonnières, and nine other towns in the area accounted for another fifty-six Breton migrants to Bonnières. The fact that the Bonnières Bretons were all from more or less the same *pays* must surely have acted as a cohesive force; shared memories, a common patois, similar habits in the most trivial aspects of life must have bound them together and furnished them with the psychological strength needed to face the challenges of adaptation to life in Bonnières. This phenomenon has been observed among other groups undergoing similar experiences with migration and settlement; Michael Anderson has pointed to the role of common areas of rural origin in binding urban dwellers in nineteenth-century Lancashire together, and Lynn Lees has observed similar strengths among the Irish poor in London during the same period.[29]

[28]The tendency of emigrating Bretons to settle where others from their region had gone before was noted by a priest in Versailles as early as 1901. "By a peculiar phenomenon," wrote the abbé Euzon, "except for servants who are required to disperse by the very nature of their work, the [Breton] workers are eager to gather together in definite places according to family, dialect, and canton." The abbé Euzon wrote in the *Bulletin de la paroisse bretonne* of November 1901, and is quoted in L. Couvreur and E. Gautier, "Les Originaires de Bretagne dans l'agglomération parisienne, 1830–1949," *Bulletin de la société d'études historiques, géographiques, et scientifiques de la région parisienne* 26 (1952):6.

[29]Michael Anderson, *Family Structure in Nineteenth-Century Lancashire* (Cambridge, 1971), pp. 151–160. See also Lynn H. Lees, "Patterns of Lower-Class Life: Irish Slum Communities in Nineteenth-Century London," in *Nineteenth-Century Cities: Essays in the New Urban History*, ed. Stephan Thernstrom and Richard Sennett (New Haven, 1969), pp. 359–385, especially pp. 376–377. Professor Lees makes a persuasive case for the idea that "consistent patterns of organization indicate the presence of a cohesive way of life in Irish slum communities" (p. 383). The same appears true for the Bretons in Bonnières.

Adding to whatever stability shared memories of life in Brittany provided were the settlement patterns of the Bretons in Bonnières. They came to Bonnières in a fashion familiar to any student of European immigration to America at the turn of the twentieth century. Single men appeared first; twenty-four men on the census of 1866 can be identified as probable natives of the Côtes-du-Nord, and they were all young and single. Seventeen of these original Bretons lived and worked on Michaux's farm; another five lived in the household of the manager of the distillery; and two young men lived in a house occupied by a young couple, possibly of Breton origin also, though not as part of their household. Most of these migrants were gone by the time of the 1876 census, although some reappeared with Breton wives. It is not too hard to imagine these young Bretons returning to their villages in the Côtes-du-Nord with stories, if not exactly of the milk and honey that flowed in Bonnières, at least with information about the very real job opportunities there. Many of their compatriots must have believed them, for they moved to Bonnières with their wives and children. The contingent of Breton-born Bonnièrois, according to the census of 1876, included many more households composed of families than the isolated couple of 1866. Of the six Breton households present only on the census of 1876, four were regular family groups, and only two were composed of single young men living together.[30] Moreover, the great majority, seven out of eight, of the Breton households first appearing on the census of 1876 and remaining in Bonnières at least until 1886 were regular family groups. The sole exception was a group of nine single workers living together, but even some of them quickly moved toward the more prevalent model of nuclear family households; by 1886, three of them were married and had begun to form their own families. More Bretons, mostly young couples, came in the 1880s and 1890s to work in the factories, and some of these new arrivals took it upon themselves to have young single Breton men as lodgers, a move that surely must have lessened feelings of culture shock and alienation among the young men.

[30]A regular family group is defined as a married couple with or without children, or a widow or widower with children.

Most Breton immigrants to Bonnières succeeded in making a living, for Breton names do not appear in disproportionate numbers on the welfare rolls of the 1865–1915 period. But poverty remained a problem for at least some Bretons. Meeting in May 1891 to draw up the budget for 1892, the bureau de bienfaisance tackled a new problem caused by these Bretons; it noted that "every year, workers from the commune, in a complete state of indigence, without resources and sometimes sick, ask for return fare home so that they can go back to their native province."[31] A token fifty francs was added to the budget to assist these workers.

Yet even in their poverty, these workers were behaving much like other Bonnièrois. Earlier in the history of the village, in the hard decade between 1846 and 1856, people faced with economic hardship left the village, often for the cities. These Breton workers were also conforming to the pattern of leaving a situation they did not like and could not change. Migration has been recognized as a factor promoting stability in rural France, as an escape valve for malcontents.[32] The Bretons who could not make ends meet in Bonnières may not have left for Paris to man barricades, but they did indirectly promote the economic and social stability of the village by taking their problems elsewhere. By leaving instead of becoming a drain on the town's resources, they permitted a better relationship to exist between their compatriots who remained and the core population. In the final analysis, it was precisely because the Bretons placed so few demands on the town that they got along as well as they did with the Bonnièrois.

The factory workers lent color to Bonnières, but they never dominated the town completely. Evidence suggests that the years after the establishment of the factories also saw the gradual *embourgeoisement* of the commercial and generally upper-class sectors of the population. The number of moderately expensive houses in the village, for example, increased appreciably between 1829, when the cadastre was first drawn up, and the be-

[31]AMB, minutes of the bureau de bienfaisance meeting of May 14, 1891.
[32]Judith Lewis Herman, "Chanzeaux under Quatrebarbes," in *Chanzeaux: A Village in Anjou*, ed. Laurence Wylie (Cambridge, Mass., 1966), pp. 55–56.

ginning of the Third Republic. Truly lavish houses remained the exception—in 1876 as in 1829, it was the notary, an exceptionally wealthy merchant, or an innkeeper who occupied a residence taxed more than ninety francs.[33] But over the fifty-year period a great increase occurred in the number of houses that can be classified as comfortable, if not luxurious, those taxed between fifty-one and ninety francs. There had been only eleven such houses in 1829, for no well-developed middle class existed to occupy them. Moreover, three of these eleven houses were owned by one very wealthy spinster who surely rented them to the transient notables of the 1830s: the bureaucrats and tax collectors who spent a few years in Bonnières before moving on to their next assignments. By 1876, however, the number of these houses had more than doubled, and almost all of them were owned by well-to-do Bonnièrois, such as Charles Hubert Boisseau, a wood merchant who sat on the town council; Mary Maloche, a grocer; Just François Allouis, a mason and future town councilor; and Jean Baptiste François Hourdou, the schoolteacher.

The increased use of domestic help is also an indication of a great degree of embourgeoisement in Bonnières. To be sure, lodgers and apprentices were nothing new in Bonnières. Throughout the century, apprentices signed up with master craftsmen to learn a trade and remained in their households for periods of one to nine years. But the position that Marie Leclair, a nineteen-year-old servant, occupied in the household of Alphonse Haquet, a grocer in Bonnières in 1906, was very different from that held by Pierre Théodore Cochet, a baker's assistant living with Pierre Nicolas Saverot's family fifty years earlier. Cochet, while learning a trade, was assisting Saverot in the bakery; Marie Leclair resided in the Haquet household for the sole purpose of making life easier for Haquet's wife.

Other changes, too, testify to the increased wealth and expec-

[33]The values at which houses were taxed were listed on the cadastre of 1829 and were updated until 1882. After 1882 a separate register was started to list house values. The post-1882 register has disappeared. Since there was virtually no inflation in nineteenth-century France, the tax values of houses in 1829 and 1876 are roughly comparable.

tations of comfort of a segment of the town's population. A piano teacher settled in the village around 1900. The shops in Bonnières at the turn of the century catered to tastes whetted by contact with urban areas. A dress store with styles from Paris offered its merchandise to women who were no longer content with the work of a host of local seamstresses. An insurance agent, a motorcycle and automobile dealer, a store carrying specialty fruits, a shoe store—all these served the needs of the more discriminating consumers in Bonnières.

The social complexion of the village, then, had been greatly altered by the passage of a hundred years. No longer a community of small farmers and rivermen, Bonnières on the eve of the First World War was a town with an identifiable bourgeoisie, an intermediate class composed of artisans and farmers, and an important stratum of workers.

These changes were not painless; they had posed problems of adjustment for Bonnières. The profusion of industrial workers at the beginning of the Third Republic had led to overcrowding, and much more seriously, the noxious vapors given off by the factories caused long and persistent protests by the villagers.

But, significantly, the outraged cries of the Bonnièrois were directed mainly against the foul air of the factories, not against the influx of newcomers who worked in them. The problem perceived by the Bonnièrois centered around pollution control, not human relations. Overt interclass friction was low in Bonnières, because of the strict limits of social integration, surely, but also because of the great escape valve of migration. Wealthy people could go to Paris to avail themselves of its many opportunities for advancement. Poor people, too, could leave the village in search of a better future in a big city. This increasingly available option of migration played a considerable part in preserving the harmony of life in Bonnières.

CHAPTER 4

Migration

The movement of people into and out of Bonnières during the nineteenth century is one of the salient aspects of the town's history. Migration played a major role in the transformation of Bonnières from a cohesive community with shared norms and expectations to a busy settlement where people's lives, concerns, and values were no longer necessarily similar. It has already been pointed out that migration served as a social safety valve, allowing discontented and impoverished people to leave the town. But migration also helped accustom the people who remained in Bonnières to the fact of diversity in human lives and attitudes, making them more tolerant, more modern, less provincial. The Bonnièrois of the 1890s was a very different person from his counterpart of 1815; he had acquaintances right in Bonnières who came from a wider variety of places, and he had greater expectations of geographical mobility for himself or a member of his family.

Even in the eighteenth century, Bonnières had never been a completely isolated town. It is difficult to measure levels of migration before the introduction of regular censuses in the first half of the nineteenth century, but as early as 1736–1745, 35 percent of the men who married in Bonnières were not natives of the town.[1] A study of the marriage contracts of the late eighteenth century also suggests that at least some young women left Bonnières in their late teens and worked as domes-

[1] This rate is typical for the period, and is in line with figures for Lourmarin, Tourouvre-au-Perche, and the three villages of the Ile-de-France studied by Jean Ganiage (*Trois villages de l'Ile-de-France: Etude démographique* [Paris, 1963]).

tic servants in such towns as Saint-Germain-en-Laye for as long as ten years before returning to their native village with hard-earned money for a dowry to marry and settle down.

Despite these evidences of population movement in the eighteenth century, it was the nineteenth century that saw the great transformations born from the possibility of migration. These transformations occurred on two levels. On the one hand, the nature of the community itself was altered; in the 1740s, the church in Bonnières may have been the scene of weddings in which the bridegroom was not from the village, but still a basic continuity of generations existed in the sense that many Bonnièrois could point to great-grandparents who had also lived in the town. By the turn of the twentieth century, this was no longer the case. The establishment of the railroad station in 1843 and the universal military service instituted after the Franco–Prussian War had made travel more familiar to the Bonnièrois, and more of them left to find work or to continue their education in Mantes, Rouen, and Paris. The industrialization of the town during and after the Second Empire also drew many people to Bonnières. The resulting population turnover was considerable, and by the turn of the twentieth century, rare indeed was the inhabitant of Bonnières who could trace his ancestry back three generations in the village.

Many French villages were transformed through migration in the nineteenth century, but the usual pattern is one of desertion and rural exodus. Three of the best village histories written by American scholars—Laurence Wylie's *Chanzeaux,* Patrice Higonnet's *Pont-de-Montvert,* and Thomas F. Sheppard's *Lourmarin in the Eighteenth Century*—all concern communities whose nineteenth-century history was one of decline.[2] Depopulation and rural exodus, however, are themes that have no place in the history of nineteenth-century Bonnières. The comparative wealth of the village beckoned people to it. The young men of Chanzeaux and Pont-de-Montvert left their native villages be-

[2]Laurence Wylie, ed., *Chanzeaux: A Village in Anjou* (Cambridge, Mass., 1966); Patrice L.-R. Higonnet, *Pont-de-Montvert: Social Structure and Politics in a French Village, 1700–1914* (Cambridge, Mass., 1971); and Thomas F. Sheppard, *Lourmarin in the Eighteenth Century: A Study of a French Village* (Baltimore and London, 1971).

Table 3. Migration to and from Bonnières, 1817–1906

Base census year	Population	Number of immigrants on next census (I)	Percent of immigrants on next census	Number of emigrants leaving by next census (E)	Percent of population that left by next census	Percent by which immigrants outnumber emigrants (P) [a]
1817	727	246	32.6	214	29.4	15.0
1836	755	261	32.5	216	28.6	20.8
1846	802	203	28.4	231	28.8	–12.1
1856	714	293	35.6	204	28.6	43.6
1866	822	390	42.0	264	32.1	47.7
1876	929	362	36.9	335	36.1	8.1
1886	980	501	43.0	354	36.1	41.5
1896	1,164	509	41.3	494	42.4	3.0

Source: Vital records and censuses of the commune of Bonnières, 1817–1906.

[a]Except for the decade beginning in 1846, when emigrants outnumbered immigrants.
P = (I – E)/E.

cause economic survival was impossible for them there. Many people, notably the Breton immigrants of the post-1866 period, came to Bonnières because of dire poverty in their home villages; yet rarely does lack of opportunity seem to be the major cause of emigration from Bonnières. To be sure, some people did leave because they could not make ends meet. On January 4, 1846, the bureau de bienfaisance voted ten francs to pay for the trip of one Madame Leclerc to Paris; Madame Leclerc, whose husband had abandoned her and her baby, was clearly leaving Bonnières in the hope of faring better in the capital. Yet, on the whole, with the single exception of the ten years between 1846 and 1856, many more people entered the village than left it.

This almost consistent excess of immigrants over emigrants is the clearest indication that Bonnières was seen as an area of economic opportunity. Table 3 gives the number of immigrants and emigrants between successive censuses, the percentage by which the immigration exceeded the emigration, and the proportion of turnover to total population. It can be seen that even before the establishment of the factories in Bonnières in the early 1860s, the net population change due to migration was usually positive. It is true that emigrants outnumbered immigrants during 1846–1856, but this difference was closely related to the economic crisis in France during the late 1840s. The decade 1846–1856 saw the only decline in population that occurred in Bonnières during the nineteenth century, although the negative migration balance was not entirely responsible. As will be shown, the excess of deaths over births in this period when cholera, among other ills, struck Bonnières was in fact twice as important as the current of emigrants in reducing the population. With the establishment of the factories, the normal pattern of an excess of immigrants over emigrants returned. The size of the surplus was closely influenced by particular developments in the industrial history of the village; thus, when a momentary dip in industrial production occurred around 1880, fewer people came to the town, and in fact the surplus of immigrants of 8.1 percent for 1876–1886 contrasts sharply with the surpluses of over 40 percent for the decades immediately before and after.

This excess of immigrants over emigrants was largely responsible for the population growth that Bonnières experienced
between 1816 and 1915. The low fertility rates could hardly
have caused an increase large enough to raise the population of
the town from 727 in 1817 to 1,231 ninety years later. Table 4
shows the respective roles of natural increase (births minus
deaths) and migration in the population growth of the village.

Table 4. Population change in Bonnières between successive censuses, 1817–
1906

Base year	Population	Natural increase (births − deaths)	Migration (immigration -emigration)	Net change	Percent change due to migration
1817	727	187 − 191 = −4	246 − 214 = 32	28	100.0+
1836	755	101 − 99 = 2	261 − 216 = 45	47	95.7
1846	802	77 − 137 = −60	203 − 231 = −28	−88	31.8
1856	714	113 − 94 = 19	293 − 204 = 89	108	82.4
1866	822	101 − 120 = −19	390 − 264 = 126	107	100.0+
1876	929	129 − 105 = 24	362 − 335 = 27	51	52.9
1886	980	165 − 128 = 37	501 − 354 = 147	184	79.9
1896	1,164	159 − 107 = 52	509 − 494 = 15	67	22.4
1906	1,231				

Source: Vital records and censuses of the commune of Bonnières, 1816–1915.

As can be seen, the positive migration balance was virtually
the sole cause of the demographic increase between 1817 and
1846. The high infant mortality rates of this period kept the
numbers of births and deaths in Bonnières approximately
equal, and it was only the influx of new people that raised the
population from 727 to 802, a gain of some 10.3 percent. This
growth rate during the constitutional monarchy is found elsewhere in the region; the much smaller population of Jeufosse
increased by 14.0 percent in this period and that of La Villeneuve–en–Chevrie rose 21.1 percent between 1806 and 1846.
These villages, located on the banks of the Seine, were relatively favored in comparison with the villages of the canton of
Bonnières situated farther away from the river; their territory
included at least some highly fertile alluvial soil, and they were
able to take advantage of the opportunities for commerce afforded by the Seine.[3] It seems reasonable to posit the existence

[3]On this question, see Richard C. Cobb, "Les Disettes de l'an II et de l'an III
dans le district de Mantes et la vallée de la basse Seine," *Mémoires de la Fédération
des sociétés historiques et archéologiques de Paris et de l'Ile-de-France* 3 (1951): 229.

of well-established currents of migration toward the Seine Valley from the poorer villages of the canton of Bonnières, and in fact, of the 207 new entrants between 1817 and 1846 whose birthplaces could be determined, some 36.7 percent were from these areas.

Population growth in Bonnières until 1846, then, followed a pattern that had parallels in the immediate region. Similarly, between 1846 and 1856, Bonnières, like its sister villages, experienced a decline in population. But the resemblance between the demographic development of Bonnières and that of its neighboring towns ends here. With the establishment of the factories, Bonnières's population soared. Lacking anything to shield them from the force of the rural exodus, Jeufosse, La Villeneuve–en–Chevrie, and Freneuse saw their inhabitants flee, unreplaced, toward Bonnières, Mantes, and the Parisian area.

Such were the major effects of migration on demographic growth in Bonnières during the nineteenth century. Who were these traveling French men and women who came to the village and left it? Some of the characteristics of the migrants changed over the course of the century, but a surprising number remained constant. One of these constants was the age composition of the people moving into and out of the village: migrants were always younger than the mean of the entire population. Throughout the century also, immigrants arrived in family groups more often than not, whereas there was a larger proportion of unattached people among the emigrants.[4] It is easy to understand why more people, especially young people, left Bonnières alone rather than in family groups; Balzac has amply described these youthful provincials lured away from their home villages by what they viewed as the glittering urban life. Marcel Sembat, born in Bonnières in 1862 and later a minister in the Viviani cabinet, is the most prominent example of a young Bonnièrois who went to Paris to seek his fortune. More typical, surely, is the case of Pierre Jean Baptiste Pattu. Born in Bonnières in 1811, the son of a postillion, young Pierre Jean

[4]According to the censuses between 1836 and 1906, between 54 and 67 percent of the immigrants arrived in family groups. Family groups, however, accounted for only 41 to 55 percent of the emigrants on these censuses.

Baptiste left his home in the Mantois for Paris, where he trained as a jeweler, and later married a Parisian.[5]

Less glamorous, but still appealing, were the possibilities open to young women for employment in other towns. In the Bonnières of the first half of the nineteenth century, women outnumbered men by six to five. How, then, could every young Bonnières girl hope to marry? One way to increase her chances was to go off and hire herself out as a servant in Saint-Germain-en-Laye, Mantes, or Versailles. There, by saving her wages, she might hope to amass a dowry large enough so that she could return to Bonnières with improved chances of marrying. Thus Marie Agathe Bonnecourt, the daughter of a winegrower in Bonnières, worked as a servant at an inn in Mantes during the early years of the Restoration. Marie Adélaïde Pichon, also the daughter of a Bonnières winegrower, put in a stint during the mid-1820s as a servant at an inn in Saint-Germain-en-Laye. Both young women returned briefly to Bonnières to get married, Mademoiselle Bonnecourt to a stableboy from Mantes and Mademoiselle Pichon to a Paris-born ropemaker. By the 1850s, Paris appears as a center of attraction for Bonnières girls. In 1857, for example, Clémentine Prévost, the daughter of a Bonnières boatman, was working as a laundress in Paris. Although she returned to her native village for her wedding ceremony, by the next year she and her husband resided at La Villette in Paris.

When women like these left Bonnières, the break was not always definitive. Many of them returned to their mothers' homes to give birth, for example; sometimes they sent their children to Bonnières, usually to the grandparents, to be wet-nursed. Their husbands might serve as intermediaries for

[5]Pattu may well have heard of the job in Paris through another Bonnièrois. In 1825, Marie Rose Langlois, daughter of Bonnières's largest native landowner and schoolteacher, married Phocien Delbouve, a jewelry manufacturer residing at 91, rue Saint-Martin in Paris. Perhaps the schoolteacher served as an intermediary between Delbouve, looking for an apprentice, and young Pattu, for when Pierre Jean Baptiste Pattu worked as a jeweler in Paris in the 1830s, he lived at Delbouve's address. This sort of detail about migrants' destinations can be found in marriage documents, which contain the addresses of witnesses; many ex-Bonnièrois returned to the town for the weddings and funerals of close relatives.

other Bonnièrois who wanted to set themselves up in Paris, and thus the contacts maintained with Bonnières served to keep the channels of movement away from the village open.

A breakdown by occupation of the migrants into and out of Bonnières shows considerable stability among the agricultural groups and great mobility among virtually all the others. Some migration did occur among the agriculturalists, although farmers and winegrowers were the least likely to leave Bonnières in family groups. Even before the decline in the importance of agriculture as a village activity, however, a steady stream of farmers' sons left the town. In fact, between 1817 and 1836, some 72 percent of the young single men who left were farmers' sons.[6] That this was an established pattern of village life is strongly suggested by the patterns of landholding in Bonnières, where the degree of subdivision was much smaller than in the neighboring village of Bennecourt.[7]

The departure of at least one son was an event that occurred in the homes of wealthy and poor farmers alike. At the top of the agricultural hierarchy of the 1820s stood such a man as Pierre Grout, a farmer in the hamlet of Morvent. Born and married in Bonnières, Pierre Grout owned 4.5 hectares in 1829, and thus was the second largest farmer in the town. His two older sons stayed in Bonnières to work his land, but their three younger brothers had left the village by 1836. A very similar transformation occurred in the household of Alexandre Boursier, a middling farmer. Like Pierre Grout, Alexandre Boursier was born and married in Bonnières. He too lived in a hamlet, Les Guinets, where he owned 2.3 hectares. His older son was still on the farm in 1836, but the younger son had

[6]Agriculturalists represented 53.3 percent of the work force in 1817 and 48.4 percent in 1836. Since they did not tend to have more children than other villagers, the figure of 72 percent implies a disproportionate number of departures among farmers' sons.

[7]According to the cadastre of 1829, Bonnières had 4,632 parcels of land for a population of about 750 people. Bennecourt, by contrast, boasted a staggering 19,775 parcels for 1,200 people. Such subdivision, of course, was in no way an asset, and the higher rate of emigration among farmers' sons in early-nineteenth-century Bonnières can be viewed as a way of dealing with the problem of land subdivision.

already left. Some men in Bonnières in 1817 had such marginal operations, of course, that no sons saw fit to remain in the village to continue farming; the one and only son of Bonnières-born Louis Pascal Côté, a landless farmer at Les Guinets, left home, as did both sons of Jean François Dumont, a gardener who owned seven ares at Morvent.

Mobility in the other occupational groups varied, but generally all the nonagricultural classes showed an enormous rate of turnover; by 1896, more than 43 percent of the town's population was composed of people who had arrived in Bonnières within the preceding ten years. Workers at the factories had the highest rate of movement into and out of the town, and the bureaucratic classes showed almost as high a rate of turnover as the workers. Every new census bore the name of a different registry clerk as well as new bureaucrats in the office of indirect taxes. The few years that most bureaucrats spent in Bonnières were clearly only a step in their careers. Their geographical origins were more diverse than those of the typical factory worker or even small shopkeeper. Cyrille Augustin Charlier, the principal clerk in the Bonnières tax office in 1866, was born in the Ardennes; Alphonse Diogue, another Second Empire bureaucrat, came from the Hautes-Alpes. These bureaucrats probably were, or considered themselves to be, of a higher social class than the majority of the Bonnièrois, for only rarely did they intermarry with the villagers. Between the comparative stability of the farming families and the extreme mobility of the factory workers and bureaucrats lay the remainder of the occupational groups in Bonnières—that is, the artisans and shopkeepers, who together usually accounted for about 25 percent of the population.

But regardless of the occupation of an entrant to Bonnières, the probability of his subsequent migration from the town was great. If only the family units entering the village are considered, and it is reasonable to suppose that they did not move away as readily as young bachelors, the percentage of family groups that left Bonnières within ten years of their arrival is striking. These figures are shown in Table 5.

Table 5. Number and percentage of family groups that left Bonnières within ten years of their arrival, 1817–1906

Year	Number of families entering	Number that left by next census	Percent that left by next census
1836	45[a]	17	37.8
1846	54	20	37.0
1856	47	20	42.6
1866	59	20	33.9
1876	80	30	37.5
1886	85	32	37.6
1896	122	59	48.4

Source: Vital records and censuses of the commune of Bonnières, 1817–1906.

[a]These 45 families entered Bonnières between 1817 and 1836; since no census was taken in 1826, it is impossible to determine just which families entered between 1826 and 1836.

Table 6. Birthplaces of immigrants to Bonnières between 1817–1846 and 1896–1906[a]

Birthplace	1817–1846		1896–1906	
	Number	Percentage	Number	Percentage
Bonnières[b]	27	11.5	23	4.7
Contiguous commune	67	28.6	37	7.5
Rest of canton of Bonnières	44	18.8	36	7.3
Mantes	13	5.6	8	1.6
Rest of Seine-et-Oise	21	9.0	68	13.8
All Seine-et-Oise	172	73.5	172	34.9
Eure	32	13.7	55	11.1
Côtes-du-Nord	–	–	56	11.3
Paris and suburbs	5	2.1	40	8.1
Rest of France	25	10.7	171	34.6
All France	234	100.0	494	100.0

Source: Vital records and censuses of the commune of Bonnières, 1816–1915.

[a]Only immigrants whose birthplaces are known are included. The 234 immigrants of the 1817–1846 period analyzed here represent 46.2 percent of the total immigrant population. The 494 immigrants of the 1896–1906 period represent 96.9 percent of the total immigrant population; this sample is large because birthplaces were indicated on the 1906 census.

[b]Throughout the century, about 5 percent of the immigrants were native-born Bonnièrois who had been absent on one or more earlier censuses. Their importance is exaggerated in the 1817–1846 section of this table because their birthplace was always identifiable.

Where did these immigrants to Bonnières come from, and where did they go after leaving the village? As the century wore on, the origins of the immigrants became more varied. It is possible to ascertain the birthplaces of 234 of the 507 new-comers to Bonnières who first appeared on the 1836 and 1846 censuses. As can be seen in Table 6 and Maps 4 and 5, the great majority of them came from the Mantois, the de-partment of the Eure, and the remainder of the department of the Seine-et-Oise. Those few entrants who had come from more distant areas had been born in departments located ex-clusively in the northern half of France. A Dutch-born one-legged former Napoleonic soldier moved into Bonnières and set up a tailor shop with his sons, but they were clearly the exception.

The proportion of immigrants from nearby regions began to fall when large numbers of migrants from the Côtes-du-Nord arrived to work on Michaux's large model farm and in his factories. This movement, which started in the 1860s, reached its peak during the 1880s. Table 7 gives the percentage of entrants to the village who were of Breton origin in five census years between 1886 and 1906.

Table 7. Breton immigrants to Bonnières, 1856–1906

Census year	Number of Breton immigrants	Percentage of all immigrants
1866	31	10.6
1876	88	22.6
1886	100	27.6
1896	68	13.6
1906	56	11.0

Source: Vital records and censuses of the commune of Bonnières, 1856–1906.

Bretons came to Bonnières in great numbers in the second part of the nineteenth century, but so did Frenchmen from other departments. By 1906, the origins of the immigrants were very diverse. At the turn of the twentieth century, only 12.5 percent of the immigrants were from Bonnières and its

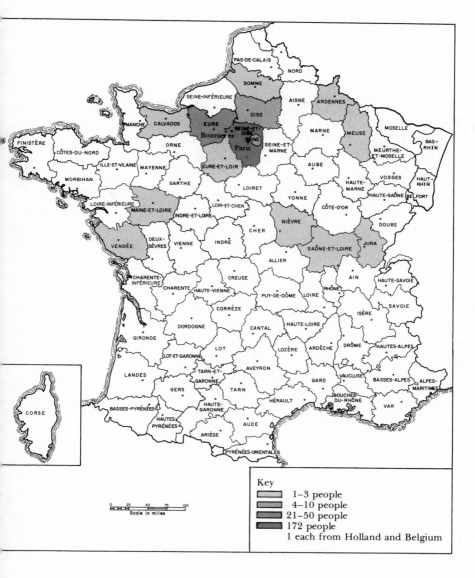

Key
1–3 people
4–10 people
21–50 people
172 people
1 each from Holland and Belgium

Birthplaces of immigrants to Bonnières, 1817–1846

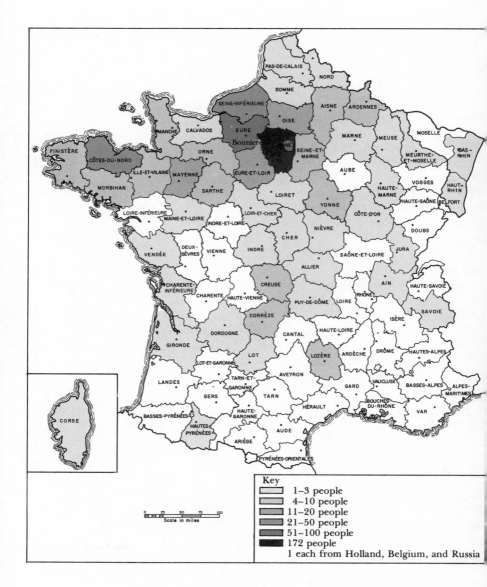

Key
1–3 people
4–10 people
11–20 people
21–50 people
51–100 people
172 people
1 each from Holland, Belgium, and Russia

Birthplaces of immigrants to Bonnières, 1896–1906

surrounding communes; sixty years earlier, this percentage had been 40.1.[8] More significantly, more than one out of every three immigrants in 1906 came from a department other than the Seine-et-Oise. Several came from poor departments in the Massif Central, which, like Brittany, experienced severe rural depopulation in the nineteenth century. Table 6 and Maps 4 and 5 contrast the origins of the immigrants to Bonnières in 1817–1846 and those of the immigrants in 1896–1906.

It is much harder to determine the destinations of people who left Bonnières. The destinations of native-born Bonnièrois who emigrated can be determined with some degree of accuracy because during the 1860s the mayor or town clerk began to make notations about the places of marriage and places of death of people born in the village. This practice became more common during the Third Republic, and thus valuable information about the destinations of some of the people born in Bonnières can be obtained.[9] The places of marriage of 461 Bonnièrois have been so determined, and are presented in Tables 8 and 9.

As can be seen in Tables 8 and 9, the proportion of people who stayed in Bonnières until marriage decreased after 1872; for women, the decline was almost 40 percent. Paris and Mantes drew more and more people over this forty-year period as emigrants from Bonnières gravitated increasingly toward urban areas. By the beginning of the twentieth century, more than one out of every four persons born in Bonnières was getting married in or around Paris. The Paris suburbs that attracted people from Bonnières were the industrialized, working-class towns to the northwest of the city: Clichy, Courbevoie, Levallois-Perret, and Saint-Denis.

But even those Bonnièrois who did not go toward the Paris area seemed to prefer urban settings. This tendency can be

[8]"Immigrants from Bonnières," a seeming contradiction in terms, refers to the few native-born Bonnièrois on each census who had been absent from the village on one or more previous censuses.
[9]Partial notations were made between 1872–1892 and 1903–1915. The 461 Bonnièrois whose places of marriage are known represent 54.0 percent of the surviving children born between 1872 and 1880, 54.8 percent of those born between 1881 and 1892, and 69.3 percent of those born between 1903 and 1915.

Table 8. Places of marriage of men born in Bonnières, 1872–1915

Years	Size of sample	Bonnières	Rest of canton of Bonnières	Mantes	Rest of Seine-et-Oise	Paris and suburbs	Eure	Other
1872–80	49	18.4%	12.2%	2.1%	16.3%	16.4%	12.2%	22.4%
1881–92	84	13.1	14.3	5.9	8.3	32.2	4.8	21.4
1903–15	110	13.6	12.7	10.0	8.2	27.3	8.2	20.0

Source: Vital records of the commune of Bonnières, 1872–1892 and 1903–1915.

Table 9. Places of marriage of women born in Bonnières, 1872–1915

Years	Size of sample	Bonnières	Rest of canton of Bonnières	Mantes	Rest of Seine-et-Oise	Paris and suburbs	Eure	Other
1872–80	39	46.1%	5.1%	2.6%	5.1%	23.1%		18.0%
1881–92	93	38.8	12.9	3.2	6.4	22.6	5.3%	10.8
1903–15	86	27.9	3.5	9.3	5.8	29.1	12.8	11.6

Source: Vital records of the commune of Bonnières, 1872–1892 and 1903–1915.

seen by the places of marriage (and often of death) of the Bonnièrois who had moved outside the ring of departments surrounding Paris by the time they married. These ex-Bonnièrois did not marry in faraway small towns, but in such medium-sized cities as Le Mans, Rennes, Caen, Rouen, Amiens, Arras, and Nancy.

By the end of the nineteenth century, then, Bonnières had become a sort of stopping place. In both 1896 and 1906, two out of every five villagers were new arrivals, and the resident who had been born and raised in the village was the exception rather than the rule. What role, one may well ask, did the whole question of mobility, the decision to migrate or not to migrate, play in the lives of individuals and of entire families?

It would be difficult to assert that emigration followed class lines. Both rich and poor left the village. Marcel Sembat, the future minister of state, went to Paris, as did the architect Jacques Carlu, who also spent ten years of his life in Cambridge, Massachusetts. But it is clear that geographical mobility had played a large role, too, in the lives of two poor and aged workers who applied to the bureau de bienfaisance for relief under the 1907 law on aid to old people. Since they had not resided anywhere for five years consecutively, they listed their various domiciles. Jean Marie Chapuis, a day laborer born in Chevilly in the department of the Oise in 1831, found himself in Bonnières in 1910, a childless widower. He had spent the year 1886 in Elbeuf, and the next ten years in Rouen. Between 1897 and 1901 he lived in Pont Audemer in the Eure and thereabouts. In 1901 he moved to the Bonnières area, where he spent time in Boissy-Mauvoisin, Rosny, Rolleboise, Saint-Illiers-la-Ville, La Villeneuve-en-Chevrie, Lommoye, and Bonnières. The life and travels of François Conversat, a day laborer born at Villettes in the Eure in 1836, present a similar pattern. For the twenty years between 1868 and 1888 he lived in the Eure: 1868–1870 at Louviers, 1871–1875 at Les Andelys, 1876–1880 at Saint-Vigor and La Madeleine, 1880–1888 at Pont Audemer. The next twenty years he spent in Bonneville, Louvrières, Chevannes, Jeufosse, Bonnières, Freneuse, Rouen, and again Jeufosse and Bonnières. Neither he nor Jean Marie Chapuis were *gens sans feu ni aveu* (vagrants). They were simply workers who moved around a lot.

Accounts of the wanderings of individual migrants are useful, but an examination of the behavior of several generations of one family furnishes a much more detailed and rich picture of the way in which villagers dealt with the option of mobility. When the Bonnièrois is viewed in the context of his family, his decision to go or to stay can be considered in light of the aggregate wealth of the family, particular catastrophic events within the family, and even the individual's order of birth. Styles of migration that have already been discussed—individual departures of young men in search of professional advancement, gravitation of villagers toward the Paris basin—can be seen clearly and put into a broader perspective when the movement of the individual is viewed in the framework of similar behavior by his brothers and sisters, his uncles and aunts.

In the story of the fates and destinations of the descendants of Jean Baptiste Saunier, the interaction of such factors as parental occupation, the distribution of limited wealth, and personal tragedy can be clearly observed. Jean Baptiste Saunier, the son of an innkeeper, was born in Bonnières in 1769. At the age of twenty-eight he married Marie Anne Clotilde Chatelain of Bonnières, whose father also owned an inn. By 1817, when the first census was taken in Bonnières, Jean Baptiste Saunier was operating his father's inn; he also had a son and daughter of his own.

The branch of the family formed by the descendants of the daughter, Marie Anne Clotilde Saunier, was the first to leave the village. By 1856, in fact, they had all established themselves in Paris; in so doing, they anticipated the general movement of Bonnièrois toward Paris by some forty or fifty years. The reasons for the early departure are not mysterious. In 1836 Marie Anne Clotilde Saunier married Jean Baptiste Prévost, a bargeman from the Eure. Did the boatman stop one day, in those times before the railroad came to Bonnières, to refresh himself at Jean Baptiste Saunier's inn, and there see the innkeeper's daughter? Or did the innkeeper himself pick out the bargeman as a good husband for his daughter, and arrange the marriage through his customers among the rivermen? Whether the marriage was initiated by proclivity or sound business sense, the involvement with mobility and transportation was already part of the world view and expectations of the children of Jean Baptiste Prévost.

And they would soon find themselves leaving Bonnières forever. The Prévosts had three daughters between 1837 and 1840, and Marie Anne Clotilde Saunier died three days after the last one, Célina, was born. Four days later, the baby, sick or starved, also died. Jean Baptiste Prévost had remarried by 1846—the surplus of women in the countryside in the first half of the nineteenth century meant that widowers rarely had trouble remarrying—but his two daughters left the village by 1856. Clémentine, the younger one, went to Paris, where she worked as a laundress, returning briefly to Bonnières in 1857 to celebrate her marriage. In 1858 she and her husband were living at La Villette.

Marie Anne Clotilde was not the only child of Jean Baptiste Saunier. The innkeeper of 1817 also had a son, born in 1800, and also named Jean Baptiste, who was to inherit his father's middle-sized landholdings, some 1.26 hectares. In the 1820s this son married a girl from nearby Méricourt. He farmed his father's land in Bonnières, for the operation of the inn was taken over by his uncle. The young farmer produced one heir, Jean Baptiste Adrien, born in 1824. This grandson of the innkeeper followed in his father's footsteps and also became a farmer. He inherited his father's land when the latter died in 1850, and soon bought more land in the village; his holdings eventually reached 6.97 hectares, not an insignificant amount for a Bonnières farmer. Jean Baptiste Adrien Saunier, much like his father, married a girl from a neighboring village, and they too had one child, a daughter, Célestine Eléanore Saunier, born in 1851.

Célestine, heir to some seven hectares of land, married Paul Poupard, a cattle and veal merchant at Saint-Ouen, in 1874. Paul Poupard's family, originally from the Mayenne, must have sunk at least some roots into the Paris area, because his two brothers who witnessed his marriage both lived and worked

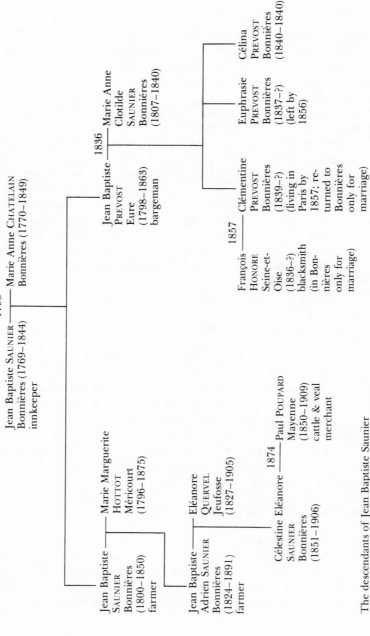

The descendants of Jean Baptiste Saunier

there, one as a tripe seller at Passy in Paris and the other as a specialty farmer in Saint-Ouen.

Paul Poupard must have been impressed by the bustling economy of Bonnières; he must have felt that good fortune was possible for him there, for he left Saint-Ouen and moved to Bonnières. There he proceeded to buy some six and a half hectares in his own name; his wife owned another seven. Paul Poupard was elected a town councilor and deputy mayor in 1896; he served as mayor between 1898 and 1900, and remained on the town council until his death in 1909.

One branch of the descendants of Jean Baptiste Saunier, then, had been gone from Bonnières for well over half a century by the eve of the First World War. But the other half, which also reached its end with the death of Paul Poupard, had managed, through careful accumulation of wealth and restriction of births, to improve its position in village society.

The general theme in the history of the descendants of Jean Baptiste Saunier is attrition, and this, it should be emphasized, was the normal pattern for any individual family in Bonnières; rare indeed was the family that maintained itself at full strength throughout the century. People migrated, as Philippe Ariès has suggested, because it was an option that lay waiting for them.[10] The call and ferment of the Paris basin attracted villagers in increasing numbers throughout the nineteenth century. Many headed for the industrial suburbs on the northern edge of Paris. The richer Bonnièrois doubtless took advantage of the capital's educational opportunities. Single girls went to serve as maids. Yet the loss of some of its citizens did not destroy the life of the community. For thanks to its industrial sector with its continual opportunities for employment, Bonnières attracted people from other areas. Bretons, residents of the more isolated communes of the canton of Bonnières, people from all over France came to replace those who had left.

Bonnières never became a bedroom suburb, however, for the days when Bonnièrois would commute to jobs in Mantes were still far in the future. The town retained its own institutions

---

[10]Philippe Ariès, *Histoire des populations françaises et de leurs attitudes devant la vie depuis le XVIIIe siècle* (Paris, 1948), p. 48.

and social life, which, paradoxically enough, functioned more smoothly because of the considerable population turnover. In the right circumstances, when competition for available jobs is not a factor, for example, contact with new people can be a great teacher of tolerance. By the beginning of the twentieth century, the people of Bonnières were well acquainted with the fact of diversity in human life. It is unlikely that a Bonnièrois would have asked Montesquieu's famous question, "How can one be a Persian?" for he had lived in a community with a Russian doctor, Spaniards and Italians, Breton laborers, and people from all over France. How this exposure to many varied life styles may have contributed to the relative social peace that reigned in Bonnières at the beginning of the twentieth century will be examined in the next chapter.

CHAPTER 5

Political and Religious Behavior

Several questions arise when we try to assess social interaction in a community like Bonnières. Was local government torn by serious quarrels? Were political questions important to the community, either as ideological issues in themselves or as vehicles for interpersonal grievances? In any nineteenth-century French town, the way the school secularization program of the Ferry government was handled is a good indicator of the degree of religious and social consensus. Were schoolteacher and priest locked in mortal combat, or had a workable level of mutual respect been reached by the town's civil and ecclesiastical authorities? The answers to these questions can go far toward elucidating the ways in which the Bonnièrois themselves responded to changes in their community.

Measured by these yardsticks, Bonnières appears as a town where a reasonable degree of social peace prevailed. The village government generally ran very smoothly. As in countless other communes in France, regimes came and went but the town council remained, swearing allegiance to each government in turn and carrying on day-to-day business. Bonnières's experience with governmental stability on the local level may have been repeated all over France, but its encounter with the late-nineteenth-century clash of the sacred and the secular was much less painful than that in many other communities.

Governmental functions in Bonnières were carried out by an amalgam of insiders and outsiders. Town councilors usually had roots in the village, but mayors, until the advent of Louis

Leblond in 1892, often did not. Between 1828 and 1874, for example, none of Bonnières's five mayors had resided in the village for even five years before assuming office. Both Louis Antoine Henri Rousselin, who was mayor between 1828 and 1840, and Paulin Courtaux, who presided over the town's affairs between 1848 and 1870, were notaries who became mayor almost immediately upon settling in the village. Similarly, two important figures in commerce, Marin Michaux, director of the post relay and father of Jules Michaux the industrialist, and Charles Victor Vermillet, a wine merchant, became mayor shortly after their arrival. Moreover, when Marin Michaux moved to nearby Cravent in 1848, he soon assumed the functions of mayor there.

For a good part of the nineteenth century, the office of mayor seemed to be an almost honorific post, given by the prefect to a well-to-do citizen in recognition of his financial status. A careful selection of deputy mayors ensured that at least one of the chief administrators of the town would be familiar with its workings; the deputies who served under these "outsider" mayors between 1828 and 1874—Jean Etienne Sembat, Jacques Charles Auguste Colin, Alexandre Tollay, Pierre Prosper Maloche, and Pierre François Chatelain—all belonged to fairly prosperous families long established in Bonnières.

Picking a comparative stranger, even a wealthy and qualified one, was something of a risk, and with Paulin Courtaux, the notary who was elected mayor in 1848, Bonnières got its hands burned. For after his death in 1870, it came to light that M. Courtaux had been quite irregular in his business dealings. The commune now found itself 2,800 francs in debt because of Courtaux's dishonesty. The Courtaux affair made the prefect, and later the Bonnièrois, more reluctant to hand over the mayoralty and the keys to the town coffers to a comparative newcomer. The mayor chosen in 1874 was Jules Michaux, the industrialist and son of a former mayor. At the time of his election he had lived in Bonnières for some thirty years. The selection of Michaux was the beginning of a new pattern; from 1874 until 1914, mayors were chosen from families that had been in the village at least twenty years, and usually almost fifty.[1]

Town councilors were generally recruited from the ranks of people who had lived in Bonnières for some time, for the tasks of a town councilor were much more mundane than the position of mayor, and yielded much less recognition. Occasionally, to be sure, men of high financial or professional stature were given seats on the town council even though their association with the village had been rather brief. Victor Celles, a businessman from Saint-Illiers-la-Ville, listed only on the census of 1846, sat on the town council from 1843 to 1848. Léon Louis Grégoire Lesieur, a justice of the peace who resided in Bonnières for a short period in the 1860s, sat on the council for less than a year, as did Ernest Etienne Verneuil, a pharmacist who lived in the village briefly during the 1880s. But these men were the exceptions; throughout the century, about two-thirds of the town council was always made up of villagers whose families had been in Bonnières more than twenty years.

It would be naive to imagine that all Bonnièrois participated in local government. The town councilors were recruited from a rather closed group. They were among the richer residents; they never included any Bretons; and many of them were united by kinship ties. Ninety-nine town councilors from the years 1815–1914 have been identified, and of these, forty-one were related to at least one other town councilor.[2] Some Bonnières dynasties produced as many as three generations of town councilors in the period; Charles Antoine Maloche, a

[1]This tendency to trust insiders is seen in the treatment of Pierre François Chatelain, the deputy mayor who had unknowingly signed papers that had severely compromised the finances of the commune. Chatelain was at first required to pay the amounts assigned to him by the Court of Appeals. He began paying, but within two years the town council of Bonnières relented. In its meeting of August 6, 1876, it voted to assume the rest of Chatelain's share of the debt, noting that "Chatelain . . . only made the mistake of having too much confidence in former mayor Courtaux." The town council could not forget Chatelain's loyalty and honesty, and especially his "twenty-five years of service rendered to the commune."

[2]Complete lists of the town councilors who served after 1838 are available in the Archives Municipales de Bonnières (hereafter cited as AMB). The minutes of the town council meetings before 1838 are lost, but three earlier lists of town councilors exist, from May 1819, September 1831, and October 1834.

winegrower in 1817, his son-in-law Pierre François Legrand, Bonnières's first schoolteacher under the Guizot law, and Legrand's son-in-law Hubert Boisseau all sat on the town council. These examples could be multiplied; the descendants of François Lechasseur, a large farmer who owned 5.7 hectares of land, according to the 1829 cadastre, included no fewer than five town councilors. And the family that produced Marcel Sembat also turned out its share of town councilors.

This government, closed in its recruitment, ran smoothly, for the Bonnièrois usually agreed with the great political changes in France. Bonnières's young men appear to have responded enthusiastically to the Revolution, for almost all of them signed up for military service in February 1792. The events of the Revolution did not spur people to try to settle long-standing local scores; Maurice Poncelet noted that "The two seigneurs of Bonnières [the seigneurs of Rosny and La Roche Guyon] were not particularly despotic; the château of La Roche Guyon had even been a center of liberal ideas for a long time; no hatred existed, and no memory of real oppression; it was in complete serenity that Bonnières made her sacrifices on the Altar of Liberty."[3]

The Bonnièrois accepted further modifications of the political structure, giving unanimous consent to the Constitution of the Year III. They welcomed the Napoleonic empire with another unanimous vote, and celebrated it properly with Te Deums for the Feast of St. Napoleon, the anniversary of the crowning of the emperor, and similar occasions. These municipal feasts, many of which took place during 1809 (to help people forget the Spanish defeat?), were somewhat quaintly recorded by Claude Delaunay, the village notary. After mass, "the people were entertained by dances and games that lasted well into the night; orderliness and decency were combined with pleasure."[4] Even though the years of rejoicing were followed, in 1812 and 1813 especially, by years of high grain prices, there is no recorded opposition to the Napoleonic regime.

[3]Maurice Poncelet, *Histoire de la ville de Bonnières-sur-Seine* (Mantes, 1947), pp. 68–69.
[4]AMB, ordinances of the mayor, August 15 and December 3, 1809.

Bonnières's support of the Revolution and Napoleon, however, did not lead to any spectacular demonstrations of fervor
or patriotism. Poncelet's comments about the mildness of the
seigneurial regime before 1789 go a long way toward explaining this complacency. Furthermore, Bonnières had no charis-
matic leader, no firebrand of revolution to goad his fellow citizens onward. The neighboring town of Freneuse did have such
a zealot in the person of François Defert, and its comportment
during the Revolution was markedly different from that of
Bonnières. Under Defert's guidance, Freneuse repeatedly sent
messages of special congratulation to the Convention; it also
sent several shipments of gold and silver and linens to be used
for the war effort.[5]

[5]Freneuse's assiduity in congratulating the Convention for various feats was
striking. In January 1794 the municipal officers of Freneuse notified the Convention that the town was sending silver, copper, iron, pewter, and other objects of value to be used for the war effort. Two months later, Freneuse praised
the Convention for "its glorious work, its energy and courage in uncovering
conspiracies, [and] charged it to remain at its post to work for the salvation and
happiness of the Republic." Six weeks later, Freneuse was commending the
Convention for its belief in the existence of the Supreme Being and the immor-
tality of the soul. And even after the fall of Robespierre, Freneuse had only
good words for the actions of the Convention. In a message of November 1794,
"the assembled citizens of the commune of Freneuse . . . congratulate the Convention on the glorious day of 10 Thermidor. Let them know, these new
Robespierres, these bloodthirsty, domineering men, that the people, by re-
covering their rights, have sworn death to him who would usurp their sover-
eignty." The quotations are from the *Procès-verbal de la Convention nationale
imprimé par son ordre* (Paris, 1792), vol. 36, p. 2, and vol. 51, p. 22.
    Throughout the nineteenth century, Freneuse kept its revolutionary con-
sciousness, thanks in large part to the radical tradition maintained in the
Defert family. Opposition to Louis Napoleon in Freneuse was overt and strong;
in 1858 the subprefect of Mantes had to dissolve Freneuse's town council on
the grounds that it was too strongly republican. And even after the establishment of the Third Republic, when reforming sentiment no longer was directed
only to political reforms but to economic questions as well, the Defert family of
Freneuse maintained its progressive tradition. When Eugène Alexis Defert
made his will in January 1889, he divided his land among his children, but he
was less concerned about ensuring precisely equal inheritances than in setting
up a logical arrangement. "If I am acting thus," he concluded, "it is to do
everything in my power to fight excessive land subdivision, which is one of the
great afflictions of French agriculture." I am grateful to Pierre Gilbert of Freneuse, the great-grandson of Eugène Alexis Defert, who showed me this will
during the summer of 1975. Bonnières, lacking similar individuals, had a less
flamboyant political history; indeed, Albert Anne does not believe it even had a
popular society during the Revolution of 1789.

The Restoration, too, failed to stir up stormy passions among the Bonnièrois. The religious missions organized in 1819, for example, never reached Bonnières, although missionary activity took place in Freneuse, Moisson, Rosny, Bennecourt, and La Roche Guyon.[6] We cannot conclude that no Bonnièrois trekked off to hear fiery preachers in these nearby communes, but their effect was surely less than that of a mission crusade launched within the confines of the village itself. Religion was not invested with new life in Restoration Bonnières, but absent, too, was the divisive, polarizing effect on political as well as religious life of a full-fledged preaching crusade.

Louis Philippe and the Second Republic also managed to win the loyalty of the Bonnièrois. We have already seen the railroad-burning incident of February 1848, an episode more noteworthy for its Luddite economic message than for any genuinely political ideas. When the constitution of the Second Republic was promulgated in November 1848, a celebration reminiscent of the 1789 Revolution was held; an altar was erected near the Tree of Liberty, streets were illuminated, and a free public ball was held, where, presumably, "orderliness and decency were combined with pleasure," although Delaunay's successor was not given to such turns of phrase.

It is only with the advent of Louis Napoleon that Bonnières's political conformity seems to sour and be transformed into something more menacing, more quietly enraged. It is important to stress at the outset that many of the data used in the following discussion are less solid than they might be, and that protest was rarely loud and overt. The town council still asserted in 1865 that "Bonnières has continually respected order and authority. . . . Its behavior is excellent and it has never done anything to disturb the peace and tranquillity that are so important for its prosperity."[7]

Nonetheless, cracks appear in this pleasant facade. Poncelet noted that a petition of 1852, presumably sent by departmental authorities asking for a popular display of support for an extension of Louis Napoleon's powers, received only the follow-

[6]Archives Départementales des Yvelines (hereafter cited as ADY), IV 8, missions, preaching, erection of crosses, 1808–1859.

[7]AMB, minutes of the town council meeting of May 13, 1865.

ing signatures: Paulice (Po-lice), Ratapoil (Naked Rat), Culotte de Peau (Fur Breeches), Bas de Cuir (Leatherstocking), Bâton (Stick), and Tape Dur (Slavedriver).[8] This petition, needless to say, was not returned to the prefect. Furthermore, seven Bonnièrois, according to the police commissioner, possessed or were passing around "an anarchistic book, containing all sorts of slander against His Majesty the Emperor." (The book was Victor Hugo's *Napoleon the Little.*)[9]

Anti-Napoleonic spirit seems to have spread as the regime continued. The police commissioner's report for November 27, 1865, contains an entry that conceivably points to a speech of political opposition. "The mayor of the commune of Benne-court," wrote the commissioner, "and one Monsieur Jean Pierre Laper, whose mental faculties are troubled, gave a gro-tesque public speech last Sunday, October 22, on the small island between Bennecourt and Bonnières. This speech, which was unbelievably silly, covered the mayor with ridicule."[10] Per-haps. But we may well wonder whether the commissioner would have troubled himself to report the ravings of a de-ranged person. A more plausible hypothesis is that an anti-Na-poleonic speech was made, that many people heard it or heard about it, and that this mocking style of reporting it was the best way the commissioner could think of to handle the situation. More drastic action might have created martyrs or heroes.

One way or another (and one way may have been the com-munal choir, or Orphéon, which was established in 1860), anti-government sentiment grew in Bonnières. The plebiscite of May 8, 1870, in which voters were asked to approve or reject the new Ollivier constitution, drew 70 "no" votes and 5 blank votes out of a total of 236 voters in Bonnières. This rate of 32 percent opposition contrasts sharply with the 17 percent oppo-sition for all of France.[11]

Why should the Bonnièrois have found Louis Napoleon so

[8]Poncelet, *Histoire de la ville de Bonnières-sur-Seine*. Poncelet's reference for this petition is simply "Documents personnels."
[9]AMB, register of infractions, entry of September 21, 1857.
[10]AMB, police commissioner's log of daily operations, entry of November 27, 1865.
[11]Poncelet, *Histoire de la ville de Bonnières-sur-Seine*, p. 78, and Gordon Wright, *France in Modern Times*, 2d ed. (Chicago, 1974), p. 149.

distasteful? Surely they had no quarrel with the prosperity that
the Second Empire had brought to their village. Michaux's expansion was due in large part to his ability to borrow money
from that Napoleon-sponsored institution, the Crédit Agricole,
and although the Bonnièrois may not have made the explicit
connection, their town council repeatedly expressed its satisfaction with the progress and trade so closely associated with Michaux. "L'Empire, c'est la paisse [baisse]" (The Empire spells
decline) may have made sense to James de Rothschild after
1859; it had no meaning for the Bonnièrois.

I suggest that the Bonnièrois found Louis Napoleon repug-
nant because they disliked his ideological stance. Bonnières may
have been a politically malleable community, able to adjust to
each successive regime, but without a tradition of severe polar-
ization, with little experience with fanaticism, the Bonnièrois
may have found Louis Napoleon, the self-conscious imitator of
his uncle, too pompous for their tastes, too eager to set police
commissioners to watch them—in short, too retrograde in a
practical era of commerce and trade.

French villages, as Laurence Wylie has shown in his work
on Roussillon and Chanzeaux, latch on to the specifics of national political programs to the extent that they strike a responsive chord in relation to local preoccupations.[12]
Bonnières, like the vast majority of French towns that supported the various regimes of the 1789–1900 period, was able
to do so when they did not offend local traditions in too
egregious a fashion. In terms of the political past of each
village, these regimes were tolerable. Bonnières's response to
the Second Empire deviated from this pattern because the
government of Louis Napoleon violated traditions, even recently formed traditions, of rationality, practicality, and tolerance for different ideological stances.

With the coming of the Third Republic, Bonnières returned
to its pattern of support for the national government at the bal-
lot box and avoidance of ideological squabbling at home. The

[12]Laurence Wylie, *Village in the Vaucluse*, rev. ed. (New York, 1964), pp. 206–
239; and Laurence Wylie, ed., *Chanzeaux: A Village in Anjou* (Cambridge, Mass.,
1966), pp. 15–71 and 258–278.

subprefect's records sometimes identify town councilors as moderates or conservatives; thus Louis Leblond, Aimable Parfait Saunier, Pierre Beaugrard, and Charles Victor Vermillet formed a conservative minority on the town council of 1881, and Ernest Barat and Eugène Couturier were clearly anticlerical in 1901.[13] Yet their positions were not rigid, and as we shall see, their behavior at town council meetings indicated a fundamental willingness to compromise. Even the subprefect was hard pressed to characterize Jules Michaux's political coloration during his tenure as mayor; basically loyal to the government, Michaux nonetheless appeared "without any clear political stance."[14]

This absence of ideological struggle, of course, does not mean that Bonnières's local political figures were incapable of artful insults and fierce verbal battles. During the 1890s, for example, the intervention of the prefect of the Seine-et-Oise was needed to get the acerbic industrialist Louis Gentil and Mayor Louis Leblond to sit down at the same table so that the town council could meet; but, by all accounts, these battles were expressions of personal conflicts with personal repercussions only.[15] The sectarian rivalries that tore other town councils apart during the years preceding the separation of church and state left Bonnières unharmed.

Throughout the century, church and state had managed to live in some semblance of peaceful coexistence in Bonnières. By all accounts, the town, which was virtually entirely Roman Catholic, was not a very devout one. We have already seen that the abbé Dutois viewed the departure of the Feugère family around 1820 as the point at which religious practice began to decline in intensity; by 1859 he was reporting that only one hundred people went to mass regularly, and not many more did their Easter duty.[16] The industrial and agricultural survey of September 1848 also noted that the level of religious educa-

---

[13]ADY, II M 29²¹, notes on the 1881 renewal elections of the Bonnières town council.

[14]Archives Nationales, F 1b II S&O 10, comments on the election of April 30, 1882.

[15]ADY, II M 29²¹, notes on the 1892 renewal elections of the Bonnières town council.

[16]ADY, II V 25, pastoral visit of 1859.

tion in the canton left much to be desired. Wealthy people continued to support the church, however; in 1845, some two thousand francs were donated for new furnishings and ornaments, and a one-thousand-franc legacy from Marie Rosalie Feugère enabled the church to enlarge its door and add a handsome new oak gate in 1852.

Despite or perhaps because of the tepid piety of the town, relations between the village priest and the schoolteacher and civil authorities were cordial. The persistent ill will and endemic hostility that characterized the relations between priest and schoolteacher in other towns appear to have been absent from nineteenth-century Bonnières. This was true in the Second Empire and remained even more surprisingly true during the troubled years of the Third Republic.

To be sure, each side would have been happier if the other had behaved somewhat differently. Abbé Dutois would have preferred that the town officials set a better example for the rest of the Bonnièrois. "It is the custom in this area," he wrote in 1863, "to give a free seat at mass to the mayor, the deputy mayor, the justice of the peace, and his clerk; I leave to others the task of judging how effective this gesture has been."[17] The town council, which was responsible for overseeing the budget of the parish council (*fabrique*), strongly urged the church to reconsider its priorities. In May 1850, commenting on "major outlays of money . . . for the purchase of ornaments for the inside of the church," the town council expressed the wish that since major repairs were necessary to preserve the western wall of the church building, "basic expenses be given priority over luxuries."[18] Again in 1852 and 1854 the town council urged the fabrique to spend its money on necessities first.

But these statements on both sides were mildly phrased, conciliatory, and polite. When a problem did arise at the beginning of the Second Empire which seemed to evoke more fundamental questions of principle, all efforts were directed toward finding an amicable, mutually acceptable solution. In 1851 it came to the attention of the town council that Pierre François Le-

[17]François Napoléon Dutois, "Monographie de Bonnières," ADY.
[18]AMB, minutes of the town council meeting of May 9, 1850.

grand, the schoolteacher, was serving as a leader of the singing in church. The mayor felt that "in the interest of the education of the children of the area [he] should immediately quit [his] salaried position as lead singer."[19] In May the request was repeated, and the teacher's need for a "complete independence of spirit" was invoked.[20] M. Legrand promised to quit singing, but by August he asked for permission to resume his role as lead singer. The town council now seemed to feel that a compromise solution was possible. Although it still objected to M. Legrand's accepting compensation, because "the payment demanded by M. Legrand would put him in a subservient relation to the priest and could dangerously compromise the esteem and liberty that a schoolteacher should have," it decided, "in a spirit of conciliation," to let M. Legrand sing, without pay, on Sundays and Holy Days.[21]

Passions never became very heated in this minor dispute; at the height of the controversy, the town council found itself reminding the church to ring the bells for the Angelus, because "the Angelus is a prayer to which the faithful should be called," proof enough that the quarrel of the town council with the church could hardly have been ideological.[22]

The relations between Legrand and the church were obviously very good; and Héloïse Lefèvre, the woman who ran the private girls' school in Bonnières from 1848 until her retirement around 1880, also had cordial relations with the priest. Abbé Poiffait, in his pastoral report of 1879, noted that whatever religious practice was left in Bonnières was "due in large part to the kindly woman who has taught school in the village for more than thirty years. By her good teaching, her example, and her true piety, she has certainly helped develop and maintain religious practice."[23]

But religious practice in Bonnières, despite the efforts of the priest and the good example of the teachers, was in serious

[19]AMB, minutes of the town council meeting of February 18, 1851.
[20]AMB, minutes of the town council meeting of May 12, 1851.
[21]AMB, minutes of the town council meeting of August 11, 1851.
[22]AMB, minutes of the town council meeting of May 12, 1851.
[23]ADY, II V 29, sketch of the parish of Bonnières prepared by Abbé Poiffait for the pastoral visit of 1879, pp. 3–4.

decline at the beginning of the Third Republic. Abbé Poiffait's picture of the parish was that of a town where the influence of organized religion was very low. Poiffait saw three broad strata in Bonnières society, and only one, the smallest, could be viewed as sympathetic to the church's goals. The first group, which Poiffait identified as some three hundred Breton workers and their families, remained totally outside the influence of the church.[24] They entered its doors only for funerals, and from the entire group of three hundred, only five adults received communion at Easter. The second layer was made up of the descendants of the old families in the area. These people, farmers or small shopkeepers, formed the core of the church community. Finally, Poiffait pointed to a group of business people, petty rentiers, and bureaucrats, none of them native Bonnièrois, and all rather indifferent to religion. Poiffait singled out the tax employees, who should have been setting a good example for their fellow citizens for special disapproval.

Abbé Poiffait did not remain passive in the face of this situation. Like his predecessors, he tried missionary preaching; assisted by a Capuchin, he effected "several rare returns [which were] very difficult to keep."[25] But religious fervor had long been on the wane in Bonnières, and such emergency measures could do little to reverse the tide.

Paradoxically, this relative powerlessness of the church to influence village society was at the basis of its good relations with the town government. Secular authority saw no threatening competitor in the church, and could afford to be tolerant toward it. Poiffait noted in his report:

[24]Ibid., p. 1. Three hundred seems like a gross overestimation of the number of Bretons in Bonnières in 1879; it is more reasonable, in light of census and other data, to place the figure closer to 150. When Poiffait referred to Bretons, he probably included all factory workers, and generally all religiously indifferent people who were not bureaucrats. Poiffait's figures are often hard to trust; for example, he stated that 900 newspapers—newspapers of a freethinking slant that he found distasteful—were sold daily in Bonnières. It is extremely hard to imagine a town of some 929 people furnishing a market of that size for newspapers. One can only hope that Poiffait's figures for religious practice were more accurate.
[25]Ibid., p. 3.

The relations between the priest and the civil administration are very good at the moment; it has always been so, for my predecessor and me. Besides, as I think I mentioned earlier, the general mentality is upright and true. Moreover, despite national trends, we have a mayor who has been able to keep a conservative majority on his council, and without having a truly religious outlook himself, he is inclined to do all the good he can as an administrator.[26]

The same mixture of lukewarm faith and toleration toward the church is seen in the town's dealings with the private girls' school during the years preceding the separation of church and state. Early in the 1890s, four nuns came to Bonnières to staff the school, which was now an avowedly religious institution. About one hundred girls attended it, and its presence did cause problems for an administration that called itself "frankly and loyally republican."[27] For when the Sisters of the Congregation of the Holy Spirit refused to register in compliance with the law of July 1, 1901, the mayor was forced to order the closing of the school. No sooner had he done so than a petition was circulated calling for its reopening. After much haggling about nuances of wording, the town council passed resolutions that noted on the one hand that "the sisters perform real services to the area by the education they satisfactorily give to more than a hundred students for no charge at all," but also that the town councilors "support [both] lay education and clerical education."[28] Defrocked, the sisters appeared as schoolmistresses on the 1906 census.

A tempest in a teapot; and there were many, some much more violent, in France at the turn of the twentieth century.[29] Bonnières slipped through this period unscathed, because the feeble influence of religion on the villagers made no one fear that the town priest would somehow be able to control people's thoughts.

[26]Ibid., p. 6.
[27]AMB, minutes of the town council meeting of July 31, 1899.
[28]AMB, minutes of the town council meeting of July 19, 1902.
[29]For two case studies of tensions aroused by the secularization laws of the Third Republic, see Evelyn Ackerman, "Chanzeaux at the Turn of the Century," in *Chanzeaux: A Village in Anjou,* ed. Laurence Wylie (Cambridge, Mass., 1966), pp. 60–69. In Chanzeaux and Saint-Lambert-du-Lattay, two villages where the Vendean tradition was still alive, separation of church and state did not come as easily as it did in Bonnières.

A skeptical society is often the most tolerant society. In fact, the municipal administration of Bonnières in the 1890s had a live-and-let-live attitude that was remarkable for that troubled period. This ability to rise above factional squabbles is evident in the town's treatment of Protestants.

There must have been several Protestants in Bonnières, for in 1898 the town council voted a lodging allowance for the Protestant minister.[30] But it is unclear how many there were, in part because of the good sense and enlightened attitudes of Mayor Louis Leblond. When asked in 1894 to supply information about Protestants in the village, Leblond snapped that he "knew of no inhabitant of the town who was of the Protestant faith [but that] he could not go around examining the consciences of the citizens of the town to do this sort of research."[31]

Sectarian passions, then, were never strong in nineteenth-century Bonnières, and the rhythm of village life was never broken by fierce ideological quarrels. The formula that ensured Bonnières's success in adapting to secularization seems clear: it was a combination of circumstances of the town's history and the conscious efforts of the villagers. Without any strong tradition of religious practice, Bonnières had no entrenched clerical faction to fight the secularization laws of the Third Republic. Moreover, since the establishment of the railroads, the Bonnièrois had seen a continuous flow of newcomers: men and women from many parts of France, Englishmen, Spaniards, Swiss, Belgians, Italians, Russians. At least one Bonnièrois had traveled abroad with his family—during the 1860s, Charles Prestreau had worked as a gardener in St. Petersburg in Russia—and returned home to serve as a town councilor. All this exposure to different points of view surely introduced some sense of relativity to the minds of the Bonnièrois. And consciously, they tried to preserve ideological peace in the town. The tone of the discussions of the town council on school policy, for example, suggests that the councilors were well aware of the limits to which they could push their colleagues. Issues were never pushed to the extreme, for what

[30]AMB, minutes of the town council meeting of May 28, 1898.
[31]AMB, ordinances of the mayor, March 1, 1894.

was to be gained if a philosophical point were won but all the people involved lost? Voltaire's wonderful passage about the British stock market comes to mind: "Go into the Exchange in London," he wrote in his sixth Philosophical Letter, "that place more venerable than many a court. . . . There the Jew, the Mahometan, and the Christian deal with one another as if they were of the same religion, and reserve the name of infidel for those who go bankrupt."[32] Bonnières during the Third Republic was similarly pragmatic, too busy with its chemical factories, its railway station, and its developing dairy industry to participate in what has been called France's last religious war.

[32]Voltaire, *Philosophical Letters*, trans. Ernest Dilworth (Indianapolis and New York, 1961), p. 26.

CHAPTER 6

Bonnières on the Eve of
the First World War

If the empress Josephine could have returned to make another rapid visit to Bonnières just before the First World War, she would have seen a town that had undergone great changes physically, economically, and mentally. With the demographic growth of the 1815–1915 period, the bourg had become more densely populated and several new streets had been created. Since its northernmost boundary was the Seine River, the bourg had no place to grow but southward, and between 1882 and 1913 four new streets—the boulevard Victor Hugo (1882), the rue des Ecoles (1882), the rue Hoche (1910), and the rue Berthelot (1913)—were carved out in the area bounded by the eastern half of the Grande Rue and the rue Gaillard. As the grid of the town became more complex, other measures were taken to modernize the streets. The Grande Rue had been paved since its construction in the middle of the eighteenth century, but in 1901 sidewalks were added to all the town's streets, and nine years later enameled street signs were installed and house numbers assigned to individual dwellings.

Many buildings, too, had been transformed over the course of the century. Although there were no clear-cut rich or poor residential neighborhoods, two discrete industrial complexes were discernible in pre–World War I Bonnières. At the eastern end of the town, the house and outbuildings that had belonged to Jean Antoine Langlois during the Bourbon Restoration had passed through inheritance to Jules Michaux. He converted them into his distillery and glue factory, and after his death Louis Gentil continued to use the property industrially. At the western end of the village was a second, larger industrial zone

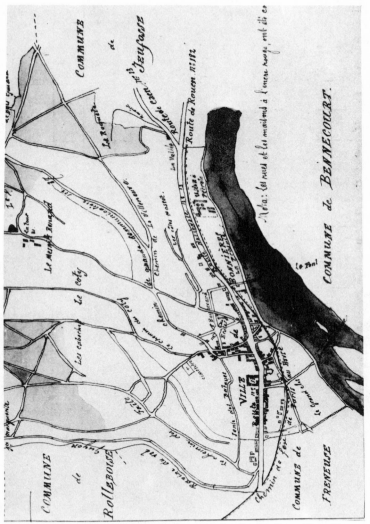

The bourg in 1899. Archives Départementales des Yvelines, Versailles

The Grande Rue around 1900

The rue Gaillard around 1900

containing the Camphre factory and the dairy plant that Ernest Colas had bought in 1898 from Louis Leblond's estate. No matter which way the wind was blowing, cynical Bonnièrois may well have remarked, the residents of the bourg could be assured of a foul industrial odor.

Industrial growth was not the only factor that changed the physical appearance of Bonnières. As the nineteenth century progressed, the village school grew, and was repeatedly moved from one temporary location to another until finally the town constructed an educational plaza in 1880. The town hall was rebuilt in 1891, and the cemetery transferred from its position next to the church to its present site on the rue Gaillard.

New residences were built in Bonnières to accommodate the growing population, which reached 1,231 in 1906. By 1886, when there were some 989 Bonnièrois, considerable over-crowding was evident on the Grande Rue, as measured by the ratio of households to houses. The census of 1846 was the first to indicate the numbers of households and houses (earlier censuses had simply listed individuals or individuals and house-holds), and it reveals an average of 1.41 households per dwell-ing on the Grande Rue. This ratio was fairly constantly main-tained until 1886, when it leaped to 1.73. Within the following decade a veritable construction boom took place, with thirty-five new dwellings constructed on the Grande Rue alone. By 1896, the fortunes of such men as Ernest Barat, the anticlerical town councilor whose masonry business employed eight ma-sons, were made, and the ratio of households to houses had dropped back to its former 1.42. Construction took place on other streets also; indeed, Louis Anquetin, writing in 1899, noted that "in the twenty-one years that I have lived in Bonnières, I count eighty-seven houses that are either new or entirely rebuilt, and in addition many repairs or major addi-tions have been made."[1] Unfortunately, we have few details on the appearance or even the value of these houses, since the building register opened in 1882 is lost, and the notarial ar-chives cannot be consulted for the years after 1852. Without

[1]Anquetin, "Monographie de Bonnières," p. 149, in the Archives Départe-mentales des Yvelines (hereafter cited as ADY).

the wealth of details that we had for the first half of the nineteenth century, we can simply echo the monographs produced
by the schoolteachers for the 1900 Exposition, which spoke
approvingly of such improvements as second floors and extra
bedrooms in peasant dwellings.[2]

Artificial lighting, both indoors and out, was another improvement. Badly lit by candlelight until the mid-1860s, rural
houses took on a more cheerful allure after the Exposition of
1867, when relatively cheap gas lighting was introduced. This
mode of illumination was perfected during the following two
decades, with the development of safer receptacles for the fuel.
The town council quickly picked up the idea of lighting the
village streets. Even before the 1867 exposition, oil lamps illuminated the Grande Rue until eleven o'clock on winter evenings when there was no moon. The number of lamps was
increased continually, and in 1903 the council decided to light
the bourg with electricity. The process of installing the wiring
was begun in 1905; an amusing entry in the town council minutes of 1906 shows that although technology can make rapid
strides, human ambition often outruns it. The electric company
was urged to speed up its work because of "numerous complaints about the electric lighting, the complaints reflecting jeal-
ous feelings rather than real need, because some areas already
have had electric lighting for several months."[3] Only the bourg
was electrified, and the discarded equipment for gas lighting
was transferred in 1907 to the hamlets of Les Guinets and
Morvent, peopled by ninety-seven citizens. Grateful for any
artificial lighting to brighten up winter evenings, the hamlets
registered no protest, and they, too, were electrified in 1915.

The commercial life of this physically modernized town had
become far more complex than it had been at the beginning of
the Restoration. From 1886 on, several "novelty" merchants
were always present in Bonnières, offering hats, dresses, and
shoes from Paris. An insurance agent made his appearance in

[2]Eugène Bougeâtre, *La Vie rurale dans le Mantois et le Vexin* (Meulan, 1971),
p. 23.
[3]Archives Municipales de Bonnières (hereafter cited as AMB), minutes of
the town council meeting of February 4, 1906.

The boulevard Victor Hugo around 1900

1896, and a local one-woman loan agency was present from 1886 on. Representatives of Paris-based commercial firms were also common features of Bonnières life from the 1890s onward. We would do well to stop and meet some of these Bonnièrois, who in their own way typify the Bonnières of the *belle époque* as neatly as the winegrowers and local notables of the Restoration represented the Bonnières of an earlier day.

The moneylender was Léontine Biraux, widow of Charles Victor Vermillet, a wholesale wine merchant who had been mayor of Bonnières between 1884 and 1892. Moneylending, to be sure, was nothing new in Bonnières, as many of the inventories after death of the pre-1850 period indicate; wealthy and not-so-wealthy Bonnièrois had long been intricately linked in a network of borrowing and lending. Nonetheless, it is noteworthy that Madame Veuve Vermillet was able to make the process of discounting notes into a full-time occupation.

The Heurteux, father and son, also did well in commerce. Eugène Arago Heurteux, a cloth merchant, came to Bonnières with his family at the beginning of the Third Republic. By 1886 he had become a novelty merchant, and by 1906 his Bonniè-res-born son Dominique had taken over the store. Dominique Heurteux must have done a good business, for his store required a clerk and his wife was able to afford a maid at home.

Perhaps the most interesting sort of commercial figure in early–twentieth-century Bonnières was the *commissionnaire,* or *représentant de commerce.* The function of this person, who became increasingly important in French business life generally in the second half of the nineteenth century, was to show samples and take orders for the wares of Paris-based companies. Bénon Cuvilliez held such a job in Bonnières during the early 1900s. He had spent some time in Paris between 1885 and 1895, had married there, and had then moved to a small town outside of Paris. From there he moved to Bonnières, farther into the hinterland, where he did well enough to have a live-in cook, even though his household included three teenaged daughters. There were three other commissionnaires in Bonnières who worked for firms located in Paris or Colombes.

This increasingly complex economy demanded more sophisticated means of transportation and communication than the quiet preindustrial Bonnières so well described by the abbé Dutois. The changes brought by the arrival of the railroad have already been described. Bicycles and a few cars also appeared in Bonnières between 1890 and 1915; many conscripts of this period listed their ability to ride a bicycle on their draft records. The 1906 census mentions an automobile and bicycle repairman, one Philippe Badaud, a Swiss who had married a Bonnières girl descended from a family of grocers. Only four conscripts of the 1887–1915 period were able to drive a car: Gaston Toutain, a mechanic who lived in Paris but was registered for conscription in Bonnières, his birthplace; Maurice Jouvet, a Paris-born mechanic who resided in Bonnières; and Marcel Delacroix and Henri Rohou, both *employés de commerce* in Bonnières. Other local drivers at the turn of the twentieth century included Dr. Rebière and the directors of the various factories. With the speed limit firmly fixed at five miles an hour, automotive traffic could hardly have been a major problem in pre–World War I Bonnières, although by 1931 the town council could talk of the highly congested streets.[4] One major advantage of bicycle riding was the time it saved young people on their trips to Mantes for business and amusement; those who could not afford a bicycle often made the trip anyway, on foot.

The years 1870–1914 saw great progress in the field of communications. Bonnières had had telegraphic service even before the 1870s; at first the railroad company had run the telegraph office but had pulled out when the volume of telegrams became onerous.[5] In 1871 the town council brought up the subject of the telegraph, repeatedly stressing its importance for trade. A letter of 1871, for example, proclaimed rather grandly, "The telegraph is progress. Bonnières, which has already assumed a certain commercial and industrial importance, will see her commerce grow even more. Commerce is life, it is work, it is well-being in our land. Therefore, let us establish the telegraph; in one way or another, we all need it."[6]

By 1874 the subprefect at Mantes had approved the commune's request to purchase telegraph service, but since the town was already taxed to its legal limit, he suggested a private collection to raise the 800–1,000 francs, or the 40 percent of the total cost of the operation, which the town was required to furnish. It is an indication of Bonnières's eagerness for telegraphic communications (or perhaps of Jules Michaux's persuasive powers) that at the same meeting the industrialist was able to announce that

[4]AMB, minutes of the town council meeting of April 17, 1931. Although Bonnières does not seem to have had any problems with delinquent drivers, the neighboring town of Freneuse caught an illustrious speeder in 1904. Claude Monet, in a letter of June 30, 1904, asked the justice of the peace of the canton of Bonnières to reschedule his hearing and pointed out that "I am completely opposed to speeding. I am extremely proud of the fact that I have never received a reprimand for speeding during the four years that I have been driving, and it is very important to me to explain this incident to you." I am grateful to Madame Calvi, town clerk of Bennecourt, for authorizing me to quote this letter.

[5]AMB, minutes of the town council meeting of November 20, 1871.

[6]AMB, ordinances of the mayor, December 3, 1871.

he had anticipated such a ruling from the subprefect and had already raised 1,247 francs from individual pledges. The telegraph was installed in Bonnières promptly.

The story of the introduction of the telephone is similar. In 1893, Jules Gérondeau, a retired notary and the son-in-law of Louis Leblond, had started urging the commune to get telephone service. A private collection was started, and the Lille-Bonnières factory and M. Rey, a notary, furnished the lion's share of the 5,000 francs that had to be raised. Several other figures in the Bonnières commercial and industrial community gave sums of two or three hundred francs: Louis Gentil, the factory owner; Marcel Sembat, the deputy; Sembat's mother; one M. Hallier, the owner of a cart rental store; Louis Leblond's son Alfred, who had followed his father into the dairy business. Dr. Rebière quickly got "le 1 à Bonnières" and Hallier "le 2." Seven other individuals as well as the town hall also signed up for phone service. Veal and cattle merchants Paul Poupard and Bruno Duval had initially shown great enthusiasm for the new telephone system, but failed to sign up for phones for themselves. Retrograde spirit or practical business sense? Probably the latter, for the farmers who supplied Poupard and Duval were hardly likely to have phones of their own. Telephone service in Bonnières was for the Mantes region only; a proposal to raise money to extend service to Paris was rejected in 1914 on the grounds that it was too expensive.

Not only did the physical appearance of Bonnières change greatly during 1815–1914; so too did its mental climate. Changes can be seen in the areas of literacy and attitudes toward education and also in the realm of what I would call possibilities for entertainment.

Literacy in Bonnières rose enormously in the decades following the passage of the Guizot law. We have seen that Langlois's school ensured a minimum level of literacy among men during the Restoration. But female literacy was extremely low; between 1816 and 1835, only 30.6 percent of the brides and 35 percent of their mothers and future mothers-in-law were able to sign their marriage acts. In the twenty years following the establishment of Pierre François Legrand's coeducational school, female literacy doubled; by 1855, three-quarters of all new brides could sign their names. By the turn of the twentieth century, over 95 percent of the new couples formed in Bonnières were literate.

No less important than the gains in literacy was the increased value accorded to education. Attendance at Legrand's school was quite casual during the July Monarchy. Between 1838 and 1849, for instance, the usual winter contingent of seventy-six pupils was reduced to fifty-eight during the summer.[7] Curriculum was limited to the three R's, with emphasis on the gospels and the catechism. It was only toward the end of Legrand's tenure, noted his successor, Louis Anquetin, that elements of history and geography were added. From mid-century onward, however, several new schools were founded in Bonnières, and their establishment reflected and reinforced a changing attitude toward education.[8] The private girls' school was opened in 1848, and by 1862 the town council was proposing the establishment of a separate communal school for girls, which would be "at least as useful as a communal boys' school."[9] Indeed, the subprefect at Mantes had to put a rein on the town council's willingness to vote funds for education, observing in 1866 that the commune was already taxed beyond its legal limit. A different financial plan provided for the construction of a new educational compound, which was completed in 1880 and housed the boys' school, the girls' school, and the newly founded kindergarten.

Nor did the town councilors' interest in education stop with the construction of the new buildings (which could have also been favored by members of the building trades for purely selfish reasons). The minutes of the town council for 1880–1914 contain many items indicating a pro-education policy: a

[7] Maurice Poncelet, *Histoire de la ville de Bonnières-sur-Seine* (Mantes, 1947), p. 103.

[8] Mademoiselle Lefèvre's private girls' school did not receive any financial assistance from the commune nor was it formally called a church school, although Abbé Poiffait thought very highly of Mlle Lefèvre. In the 1890s the school was staffed by the Sisters of the Congregation of the Holy Spirit. The communal girls' school was formed in 1865, and a public kindergarten was founded in the late 1870s.

[9] AMB, minutes of the town council meeting of November 17, 1862.

desire for an assistant teacher when the number of students should warrant one, a plea that a maid be hired so that students would no longer have to waste class time sweeping the classroom, a purchase order for laboratory equipment (test tubes, beakers, funnels, chemicals, and so forth) for both the boys' and girls' schools. Especially telling is an entry of 1888 in which the idea of education as a necessity and not a frill comes through very clearly. In 1888 the canton of Bonnières was asked to appropriate money for prize books for students who had received the primary-studies certificate; Charles Victor Vermillet, the mayor, objected to the philosophy of education implicit in that procedure, stating that "the examination for the primary-studies certificate is no longer a contest in which the pupils hope to win a prize, but rather an examination through which they try to acquire certification . . . [they are] sufficiently rewarded when they manage to gain this title . . . in that case, the prize has only a minor value."[10]

Instead of providing these graduating students with a superfluous reward, the town council voted to distribute prizes to the children who were still in school, as a reward for a good year's work and especially as motivation for their future studies. Schooling was now seen as a key to advancement and success, an end desired by parent, teacher, and child. And with justification. Would not Bonnières-born Jacques Carlu, son of a road inspector, rise to international fame as an architect? One wonders how often he and Marcel Sembat, that other Bonnièrois-made-good, were cited as examples to the town's schoolchildren on the eve of the First World War.

This increased respect for the value of education carried over into the field of adult instruction, although progress here was less smooth, perhaps because adults cannot be forced to go to school. In 1863 the town council allotted thirty francs to start a communal library in one of the closets in the town hall, and although the notion of a library in a closet may seem amusing today, here, perhaps, was the beginning of the town's careful attention to the preservation of its records. Two years later,

[10]AMB, minutes of the town council meeting of June 2, 1888.

Jean Baptiste Hourdou, Legrand's successor, opened classes for adults, held between eight and ten o'clock in the evening. According to the notice that Hourdou had placed in the town records, "Several times a week there will be lectures on the most basic sort of knowledge: on geography, history, hygiene, jurisprudence, in short, on everything a citizen should know under the reign of universal suffrage."[11] The class was free and attracted forty-two people; for his work, Hourdou received a prize from Louis Napoleon.[12] The initial enthusiasm faded, however, and in 1871 the mayor "noted with sadness that the courses for adults are undersubscribed."[13] The evening classes must have died down during the early years of the Third Republic, for in 1894 the town council spoke of reestablishing them. The teacher now was Louis Anquetin and his enrollment was about twenty pupils. Bonnières's experience with adult education was similar to that of its neighboring villages, though slightly more successful. Jeufosse, for example, experimented with adult education courses between 1872 and 1883, but had to drop them because no one came.[14]

Perhaps one reason that organized adult education never aroused enormous enthusiasm was the increasing number of possibilities for other, more informal sorts of entertainment and mental stimulation.[15] The Société des Conférences Populaires, organized in Bonnières around 1910, seems to have had considerable success. It sponsored two or three public lectures a year, which drew between 250 and 300 people.[16] Topics included such exotic fare as the society and economy of Madagascar; this lecture was given in 1910 by a guest speaker from Paris, who supplemented his remarks with slides and anti-German comments that were met with great approval by the audience.

Musical activities also flourished in Bonnières. In 1860 Jean Baptiste Hourdou founded the Orphéon, a choral society that

[11]AMB, ordinances of the mayor, October 1865.
[12]AMB, minutes of the town council meeting of October 28, 1866.
[13]AMB, ordinances of the mayor, November 20, 1871.
[14]Pierre Ernest Géry, "Monographie de Jeufosse" (ADY, 1899), p. 139.
[15]On the importance of unplanned entertainment in French village life, see Laurence Wylie, *Village in the Vaucluse*, rev. ed. (New York, 1964), pp. 304–307.
[16]Anquetin, "Monographie de Bonnières," p. 174.

may have been a hotbed of antigovernment sentiment during the Second Empire. Twenty years later, the Fraternelle, another musical group, was established; by 1913 it was offering free classes in solfège and instrumental performance. Jules Prestreau, the son of Charles Prestreau, the fancy gardener who had been to Russia, gave instruction on stringed instruments, and Victor Marchand, a farmer who lived in the bourg, gave lessons on brass.

The Fraternelle played regularly at musical events, and if we can judge by the information Bonnières's young men put on their conscription records, there must have been a considerable number of musicians in the town. (Or was it considered advantageous to point out one's musical abilities to the army?) Of the 249 young men in the classes of 1887–1915, 44, or about 1 in 6, could play a musical instrument, mostly brass and woodwinds. This seems like a fairly large contingent of musicians, and we have no information on the musical ability of older Bonnièrois. Since only one of the conscripts (Marcel Gérondeau, the notary's son) played the piano, we may assume that most of the piano teacher's students were young women. Generally, music seems to have been a part of the lives of many more Bonnièrois of the Third Republic than it had been some generations earlier; the only indication we have of musical activity in Bonnières before 1850 is the mention of some violin-playing done by Palmantier at several municipal celebrations during the Napoleonic era and the listing of violins among the personal effects of Jean Pierre Mouchard and of Marie Jeanne Ortillon, both storekeepers who died in 1828.

Musical activity, especially with the relatively large variety of instruments found in the Bonnières of the belle époque, is obviously tied to a certain level of wealth. And involvement with some sorts of music also helps individuals become aware of a culture that is removed from their immediate concerns. When Jean Pierre Mouchard played the fiddle at a wedding during the 1820s, he was fulfilling a traditional role. He had learned his tunes from another fiddler; he probably did not read music. But when the Fraternelle gathered together to play band music, some formal knowledge was necessary; horns, bugles, piccolos, and clarinets cannot be played together without direction, structure, and discipline. Learning the music, learning how to play compositions that were not passed down from father to son but rather came into Bonnières on printed paper, expanded people's horizons in much the same way as a lecture on Madagascar.

Other aspects of life in Bonnières, however, remained hermetic. The Bonnièrois were not avid newspaper readers; indeed, there were few local papers available until the 1870s. The first local newspaper in Mantes, the *Journal judiciaire; annonces et avis divers de l'arrondissement de Mantes,* had been founded in 1823, but its high subscription price and commercial nature made it of little interest to most Bonnièrois. By 1875 it was renamed the *Journal de Mantes* and sold in single issues. A second rival paper, *Le Petit Mantais,* was established in 1880, and a third, *Le Semeur de Mantes,* came into existence in 1907, but none of these papers had a great following in Bonnières. Indeed, according to Albert Anne, when people read newspapers, it was for their entertainment value, as a supplement to the *veillées* of the pre-1870 era, perhaps, rather than for their treatment of national or international issues:

People rarely bought newspapers, except when there were extraordinary crimes or adventures, such as the exploits of the Bonnot gang around 1908–1909. Then, entire families would gather in someone's house, in the evening by the fireside, for during the day there was no time to spare. And there, by the light of a candle or a petrol lamp, they would read aloud the thrilling stories that would produce cries of horror. Later in the evening, people would be very careful about bolting their doors.[17]

The Bonnièrois may have invested in newspapers mainly to follow events that were sensational or amusing; yet the outside world and the weight of foreign politics affected them in ways they could not control. The Bonnièrois may not have read all the news stories about deteriorating Franco–German relations, but the national effort to prepare for another war touched their town. From the early 1870s on, the central government

[17]Albert Anne, personal communication, June 29, 1977.

sponsored inventories of all the horses and other draft animals, and beginning in 1894, the quantities of basic foodstuffs in each commune were also counted each year. The school curriculum put a new stress on physical education in the prewar years. In July 1909 the town council made plans to build a gymnasium, pointing to its "general utility . . . from the standpoint of the military education of our youth and of national defense."[18] The gymnasium was completed in 1911, a year after the Union Sportive Bonnièroise, a voluntary association, was formed. In 1912 M. Dennel, the schoolteacher and vice-president of an organization called the Association Amicale et de Préparation Militaire de Bonnières-sur-Seine, asked permission to teach target practice after school, and it was granted.

In 1914 the war finally came, and it was far worse than any of the previous invasions that Bonnières had experienced. In May 1814 Bonnières had been required to lodge and feed a hundred-man detachment of Polish light cavalry; the next month nine thousand members of the Russian Imperial Guard crossed Bonnières in a single day in the course of their travels from Mantes to Evreux.[19] A half century later, a second invasion came when three to four thousand Prussians entered Bonnières on October 4, 1870, demanded lodging for themselves and their horses, and spent the night, only to burn the railroad station the next day.[20] The devastation brought by the First World War, however, far exceeded these earlier incidents, and, indeed, is beyond the chronological and conceptual scope of this study. The Bonnières that we shall leave is the Bonnières of early 1914—partially industrialized but free from crushing social problems, filled with commercial activity, a town of sturdy, literate people of varied origins, decent, tolerant, and practical.

[18] AMB, minutes of the town council meeting of July 1, 1909.
[19] Poncelet, *Histoire de la ville de Bonnières-sur-Seine*, p. 72.
[20] AMB, schoolmaster's report on the passage of the Prussians through the commune of Bonnières, March 3, 1871.

AFTERWORD

Why Village History?

Why write another village history, and indeed, why should microhistory be written at all? As I write these lines, I see some of "my" villagers of nineteenth-century Bonnières: Jacques Etienne Maloche, a farmer, strolling down the Grande Rue in the 1830s dressed in his feast-day best of calico shirt, silk hat and tie, black vest, and blue pants. I see Gabriel Noinville, a tailor, and his wife, Marie Madeleine Côté, eking out a living in the hamlet of Les Guinets during the Restoration, wondering how to provide for their deaf-mute son after they die. And then there are the Breton laborers: Pierre Bienvenu, for example, who came to Bonnières in the early 1870s to work in Michaux's factories. Life in Bonnières started off hard for him; he lived with eight other Breton factory workers in a cramped dwelling on the Grande Rue for several years before he married Françoise Le Hégarat, also from the Côtes-du-Nord. But then things must have looked more hopeful as he watched his children obtain jobs they never could have had back in Brittany. His eldest son, Victor, received his *certificat d'études* in 1895 and became an *employé de commerce;* his youngest son, Marcel, became a mechanic. And I think of Dominique Heurteux, the second generation of his family to direct the prosperous store his father had built up on the Grande Rue. Dominique was to march off and die, along with his brother Bernard, in the First World War, their deaths a bitter reminder that outside forces could ruin a father's hopes.

Here, perhaps, is one reason to study village history. More than any other approach, it reintroduces real, identifiable com-

161

mon folk into history. Within the last two decades, cliometricians, especially historical demographers, have invented ingenious ways to bring the behavior of large groups of ordinary people to our awareness. By careful analysis of parish registers and close work with censuses, French, English, and American demographers have created a whole new stratum of historical investigation. Patterns of marriage and fertility have become clear; seasons of death can be identified. Mute masses of people have been given a historical existence. We now know the main demographic facts of many peasant lives, even though the other details of these lives are absent.

It is the function of microhistory to restore some of these details. The advantage of studying a small community, one whose population hovers around a thousand, is that it enables us to remember individual villagers, to think about the scope and shape of particular lives. What is lost in statistical base, and there certainly is a loss, is made up in the opportunity for reflection about personal reactions to the parameters studied. It is well and good, for example, to analyze patterns of infant mortality statistically, but it is something of a very different order to be confronted with a *fiche de famille* (the form devised by the Institut National d'Etudes Démographiques for the results of family reconstruction) for the Jacques Gosselin household which shows four stillbirths and three infant deaths out of nine pregnancies occurring between 1812 and 1820. This is admittedly an extreme case, both in the frequency of conceptions and the high stillbirth rate, but nonetheless it happened, and we are faced with the problem of trying to fathom the response of the parents, who were not especially old or especially poor, to this situation. Similarly, computer printouts can indicate a great deal about trends in migration to and away from an area, but it is only by careful examination of the particulars of an individual case history that we can begin to appreciate the human dimension, the economic and psychological costs and gains, behind a decision to relocate.

These reflections suggest that there are two rather different levels at which we can try to understand the lives and motivations of village people of the past. On the one hand, there is the enticing but difficult area of their mental life: their imagination and aesthetic sense, their embryonic ideas about politics and society, their emotional reactions to *les grands événements de la vie.* There is also the more accessible area of their vocational goals and options. When, for example, did they begin to see the world as more open, more willing to respond favorably to their efforts to improve themselves and their economic conditions?

Let us begin with the first area for investigation, the imaginative, intellectual, and emotional life of the nineteenth-century Bonnièrois. These villagers do not reveal much to us about their personal tastes. The inventories after death of the pre-1852 period furnish some information, but it is hard to determine whether possessions indicate an adhesion to custom and style or a real expression of individual judgment. A modern reader is surprised, in perusing the inventories of all but the poorest Bonnièrois, to note the large proportion of wealth devoted to the family beds, especially the parents' bed, and their accessories. Peasants who possessed only two or three changes of clothing regularly had imposing canopied beds and well-stocked linen closets. But this was simply the prevailing style in the Mantois; Eugène Bougeâtre describes peasant beds as "veritable monuments," and Albert Anne, recalling the beginning of the twentieth century, speaks of visits to households where the linen closets were opened wide for viewing, to inspire admiration in the guests.

Other items from the inventories, however, suggest the barest outlines of a personal sense of style among some of the Bonnièrois. The most striking case is the clothes of Marie Rosalie Palmantier, who died in 1849, the wife of farmer Augustin Langlois (no relation to schoolmaster Jean Antoine Langlois). The household was not especially wealthy, and indeed, 1849 was not a good year for anybody. Madame Langlois, then, was not a woman with money to indulge her whims. Nonetheless, it is clear from the list of her possessions that like most Bonnièrois she liked bright colors, and more particularly, she adored flowers. Her crockery was a flower pattern against a white background; most Bonnièrois of the time had plain dishes. Her bedspread and the curtains surrounding her bed were red with green and lighter red flowers. She had a gray dress with red flowers and a darker gray dress with red and green flowers. Among her outer garments were a violet silk jacket with multicolored flowers, a black shawl with red flowers, and a muslin shawl with red and yellow flowers.[1] Nobody else in Bonnières showed such fidelity to any one motif, except perhaps the much wealthier Foissys of the Restoration, whose home and wardrobes featured much toile de Jouy.

What can we make of this and other isolated items that indicate attention to style and detail? Jean Baptiste Hilaire Moussard, for example, a cobbler who died in 1847, had fully 140 wooden forms for making shoes, as well as a large stock of assorted leathers, suggesting that those Bonnièrois who bought shoes during the July Monarchy expected nicely crafted products. What seems clear in both cases is that limited wealth did not prevent people from cultivating a sense of the beautiful, of enjoying small aesthetic pleasures. They left us few specific details, but those few are telling.

The Bonnièrois were not much more generous in recording their ideas about politics and society for us. Certainly, they never debated these issues abstractly at town council meetings. Yet their actions, in the town council and in their daily lives, suggest a people who were practical, tolerant, and above all, interested in doing what was good for business and the prosperity of the town. A resident of the neighboring town of Freneuse, Eugène Alexis Defert, did write a short political testament at the beginning of the Third Republic, and although he belonged to a family with a tradition of progressive political

---

[1]Jules Michelet had women like Madame Langlois in mind when he described the effect of technological progress in the textile industry on the lives of the poor: "Machine production . . . brings within the reach of the poor a world of useful objects, even luxurious and artistic objects, which they never could reach before . . . the great and fundamental revolution has been in cotton prints. . . . Every woman used to wear a blue or black dress that she kept for ten years without washing, for fear it might tear to pieces. But now her husband, a poor worker, covers her with a robe of flowers for the price of a day's labor. All the women of the people who display an iris of a thousand colors on our promenades were formerly in mourning" (*The People,* trans. John P. McKay [Urbana, Chicago, and London, 1973], p. 44).

attitudes, his thoughts seem fairly representative of Bonnières opinion in the 1880s.[2] An ardent republican, Defert took great pleasure in seeing the tricolor for the first time, after the Revolution of 1830. The Revolution of February 1848 moved him greatly; "joy was on all faces," he wrote, "people fraternized and planted liberty trees in even the smallest hamlets." Vigorously opposed to Louis Napoleon, Defert lamented the "coup d'état of December 2, 1851, [when] everyone was sad. We were stupefied and frightened. It was as if our beautiful, liberal, and generous France were seized by the throat and placed under a lead cover." And the Revolution of September 4, 1870, pleased him, for it marked the "return of the republic that had been ravished from us."[3] Defert's comments sound slightly stereotyped, perhaps, but still sincere: the Bonnièrois who persistently voted for government candidates during the Third Republic would surely have agreed with the broad outlines of this version of recent French history.

What can we know of the emotional life of the Bonnièrois? Here, too, they reveal very little directly. To help us, there are the well-honed tools and tests of classical historical demography, which yield data showing the declining age of women at first marriage, the introduction of contraception, the rise, albeit slight in the case of Bonnières, in the number of illegitimate births. The first two of these trends suggest that marriage was increasingly viewed as a sentimental as well as a business undertaking. In addition, there is the heightened value accorded to education, which suggests that childhood, too, must have been increasingly respected and cherished in the nineteenth century. But whether the Bonnièrois themselves were aware of these changes, whether they thought of certain ways of interacting as modern and of others as backward, we will never know for certain, until, perhaps, a new generation of historians, continu-

[2]The Defert family's contributions to political life in nineteenth-century Freneuse are discussed in chap. 5, n. 5. The Deferts appeared radical during the Second Empire, but by the 1880s most farmers in the Mantois had moved toward the views the Deferts had held earlier. For more general remarks on this progression, see Eugène Bougeâtre, *La Vie rurale dans le Mantois et le Vexin* (Meulan, 1971), p. 175.

[3]Political recollections of Eugène Alexis Defert, kindly lent to me by Pierre Gilbert of Freneuse.

ing the sensitive work of Jean-Louis Flandrin and Philippe
Ariès, devises a way of deducing thought from actions.

It is much easier for us to trace the changes in the vocational
expectations of nineteenth-century Bonnièrois. Living so close
to Paris meant that the option of migration was always open to
them. Yet it appears that the quality of migration changed after
1870; at this point, most Bonnièrois were literate, and a move
to the capital or one of its suburbs often meant a job in commerce or even in an office. In the first half of the nineteenth
century, young Bonnièrois who left often went into domestic
service or artisanal jobs in such places as Saint-Germain-en-
Laye, Mantes, and Versailles. After the 1860s and 1870s, the
Bonnièrois became part of the manpower that helped develop
and transform the greater Paris area. In a more personal sense,
too, these moves were steps in development and growth; being
a blacksmith in Versailles in 1852 was probably not so different
from working at that trade back in Bonnières. But by the
1870s, the Bonnièrois had been exposed to the process of economic change right in their own village. By seeing Michaux
transform the economy of Bonnières, the villagers must have
picked up—even subconsciously—the notion that men and
women could change their fate, especially the economic circumstances of their lives or those of their children. And so a
dual process was set in motion. Some Bonnièrois left in search
of these opportunities for advancement. Those who stayed participated in an economy that had become increasingly complex.
Local shopkeepers worked for themselves, but alongside them
(and competing with them) were representatives of Paris-based
firms. Peasants, to use Robert Redfield's phrase, became farmers; agriculture became a business, not a way of life or a view of
the world. The many small agriculturally based industries in
Bonnières on the eve of the First World War are ample proof
that the Bonnièrois were able to make this adjustment.

The Bretons shared this mentality. After all, they had come to
better themselves and had taken unaccustomed work in
Bonnières's factories in order to do so. By the turn of the twentieth century, many of them had become less distinguishable from
the other Bonnièrois than their predecessors had been twenty

years earlier; they, too, opened up small shops or took commerce-related jobs; their children also earned certificats d'études. It might be foolish to wax eloquent over Bonnières's role as a melting pot and as a center of economic opportunity; the village of Bonnières, after all, was hardly New York City. All the same, it is reasonable to view Bonnières as an open society that nurtured people until they were wise enough in the ways of the world to join the great mass of Frenchmen who clustered in the Paris suburbs in the 1910–1930 period.[4]

Village history, then, helps us see the interplay of individual lives and economic development in a very specific way. We may never be able to know whether Marie Anne Clotilde Saunier thought that she was going to die in childbirth in 1840 (the statistics, after all, were against it—but did she know that?); but we can guess, with some hope of accuracy, the reasons her older daughters felt compelled to leave Bonnières shortly thereafter. Village history also helps us understand the patterns of development of the community itself, as well as the individual lives within it. In the nineteenth century, the village of Bonnières had a brutal choice: "to change and in changing die; or not to change, and risk a swifter death."[5] The village chose change, or rather, change was foisted upon it, but once the main features of Michaux's enterprises were laid down, the town councilors and the Bonnièrois dealt competently with it.

The story of the industrialization of Bonnières leads to several reflections on the way communities adapt to change. If the transformation is too fast or too severe, even the most enlightened administrators stand helpless. It is precipitous growth, rather than the mere fact of growth itself, that often brings

[4]The migrants in Chanzeaux tended to move several times, each time to a larger town (Laurence Wylie, ed., *Chanzeaux: A Village in Anjou* [Cambridge, Mass., 1966]). Few people moved directly from a tiny village to Paris. Similarly, Bonnières served as an intermediate stop for many people who eventually settled in the Paris area.

[5]David S. Landes, "French Business and the Businessman: A Social and Cultural Analysis," in *Modern France: Problems of the Third and Fourth Republics,* ed. Edward M. Earle, 2d ed. (New York, 1964), p. 353. Professor Landes's remarks were made in connection with French business life, but they are equally poignant when applied to the problems of the nineteenth-century countryside.

with it serious problems in maintaining public order and acceptably harmonious human relations. Louis Chevalier has shown how the extremely rapid rate of change in Paris in the first half of the nineteenth century greatly intensified the usual problems of urban growth, and rapid change is no less disruptive in towns the size of Bonnières.[6] At the end of the nineteenth century, many communes near Paris underwent rapid demographic expansion. The town of Bezons, eight miles northwest of Paris, saw the beginnings of industry in the Second Empire, much as Bonnières did. But Bezons, largely because of its proximity to Paris, grew much more rapidly than Bonnières, so that its population, which numbered 834 in 1866, had more than tripled by 1896. Such precipitous expansion left Bezons with social tensions that it carried into the twentieth century.[7] Bonnières, farther off in the countryside, experienced the industrialization but not the unbounded demographic growth; population rose in Bonnières from 822 in 1866 to 1,164 in 1896, a gain of only 42 percent.

The transformation of Bonnières between 1815 and 1914 proceeded in a relatively smooth manner because of a conjunction of fortunate circumstances, the most important of which was precisely this slow pace of change. The construction of the railroad station in the early 1840s was followed by a twenty-year respite from major innovations. The burgeoning industries of Bonnières grew slowly, never overwhelming the town. Industrial workers always made up less than 25 percent of the work force, and Bonnières always maintained a middle-class element and a farming population too.

Expansion took place gradually in Bonnières largely because of its distance from Paris. Indeed, location was a key factor in determining the nature of a rural French commune's experience in the nineteenth century. Those towns that were buried too far in the countryside—Chanzeaux, which Laurence Wylie's research team studied, or Pont-de-Montvert, whose history Patrice Higonnet has analyzed—stood no chance of reaping any

---

[6]See Louis Chevalier, *Classes laborieuses et classes dangereuses à Paris pendant la première moitié du XIXe siècle* (Paris, 1958).

[7]See Jean-Pierre Hoss, *Communes en banlieue: Argenteuil et Bezons* (Paris, 1969).

benefits from the transportation revolution of the nineteenth century. Indeed, the railroads could only facilitate a swifter exodus of their youth. On the other hand, communes situated very close to Paris could not maintain a controlled rate of growth once the rush to develop the greater Paris region was on. Bezons—not to speak of Saint-Denis, Aubervilliers, and Pantin—was in this position at the end of the nineteenth century. Deserted by the middle class, these communes quickly became industrial ghettos.

Bonnières was fortunate. Being somewhat removed from the immediate Paris agglomeration, it was sheltered from the full force of the pressures that transformed many Paris suburbs from bucolic villages to dirty, overcrowded cities within thirty years. It is only today that newspaper editors in Mantes-la-Jolie, writing of the future of the area, invoke the cautions of the environmentalists and cite the need to restrain the rate of growth of the Mantois and the region around Bonnières.

Bibliography

The entries in the bibliography are divided into two main categories: primary sources and secondary sources. Within this broad classification, the following subdivisions are made:

I. Primary sources
   A. Archives Municipales de Bonnières
   B. Archives Notariales de Bonnières
   C. Archives Départementales des Yvelines
II. Secondary sources
   A. General works
   B. Works on the Seine-et-Oise and the greater Paris area
   C. Works on Bonnières and the Mantois

The most important single source for this study was the records found in the municipal archives of Bonnières. These records are not classified according to any formal scheme, and therefore they are simply listed below.

I. PRIMARY SOURCES

A. Archives Municipales de Bonnières

1. Civil register, 1816–1915; and secondarily, Catholic register, ca. 1700–1792, and civil register, 1793–1815.
2. Censuses 1817, 1836, 1846, 1856, 1866, 1876, 1886, 1896, and 1906.
3. Minutes of the meetings of the town council of Bonnières, 1838–1915. (The minutes of the meetings of the 1816–1838 period have been lost.)
4. Register of the ordinances of the mayor of Bonnières, 1800–1820 and 1838–1915.
5. Register of the deliberations of the bureau de bienfaisance of Bonnières, 1848–1915.
6. Military censuses for Bonnières, 1887, 1891–1895.

7. Cadastre of Bonnières, 1829.
8. Annual agricultural surveys for the commune of Bonnières, 1848–1915. Similar data are also available in tabular form for all the communes of the canton of Bonnières.
9. Industrial and agricultural survey, September 1848. The answers to this survey cover conditions in the entire canton of Bonnières, but are nonetheless very useful.
10. Police commissioner's log of daily operations, beginning January 1, 1865; register of infractions, also from the Second Empire.
11. Unclassified communal records on industry in Bonnières.
12. Unclassified communal records on roads in Bonnières.

B. *Archives Notariales de Bonnières*

Fonds Delaunay, 1806–1819
Fonds Robert, 1819
Fonds Rousselin, 1819–1840
Fonds Boucher, 1840–1852

C. *Archives Départementales des Yvelines*

Grain prices
II M 1–14 Grain prices at the market of Mantes, 1808–1894, 1905–1915.

Politics
II M 28[14] Elections to the town council of Bonnières, 1800–1873.
II M 29[21] Elections to the town council of Bonnières, 1874–1924.
II M[2–4] Electoral lists, 1809–1837.
II M 11[9–15] Elections of deputies, 1871–1914.

Religion
II V 25   Pastoral visit to the church at Bonnières, 1859.
II V 29   Pastoral visit to the church at Bonnières, 1879.
II V 30   Pastoral visit to the church at Bonnières, 1880.
II V 32   Pastoral visit to the church at Bonnières, 1882.
IV 8   Missions, preaching, erection of crosses, 1808–1859.

Public health
VII M 49   Cholera epidemic of 1832.
VII M 52   Cholera epidemic of 1849.
VII M 56   Miscellaneous epidemics.
VII M 57   Miscellaneous epidemics.
VII M 78   Vaccination.
VII M 79   Vaccination.
VII M 80   Vaccination.

Communal monographs
    All towns in the arrondissement of Mantes, plus Argenteuil, Bezons, Corbeil, Essonnes.

II. SECONDARY SOURCES

A. General works

Ackerknecht, Erwin Heinz. "Anticontagionism between 1821 and 1867." *Bulletin of the History of Medicine* 22 (1948): 562–593.

———. "Hygiene in France, 1815–1848." *Bulletin of the History of Medicine* 22 (1948): 117–155.

———. *Medicine at the Paris Hospital, 1794–1848.* Baltimore, 1967.

Allem, Maurice. *La Vie quotidienne sous le Second Empire.* Paris, 1948.

Anderson, Michael. *Family Structure in Nineteenth-Century Lancashire.* Cambridge, 1971.

Ariès, Philippe. *Histoire des populations françaises et de leurs attitudes devant la vie depuis le XVIIIe siècle.* Paris, 1948.

Baudrillart, Henri Joseph Léon. *Les Populations agricoles de la France.* Vol. 2. Paris, 1888.

Beaver, M. V. "Population, Infant Mortality, and Milk." *Population Studies* 27 (1973): 243–255.

Bergues, Hélène, et al. *La Prévention des naissances dans la famille: Ses origines dans les temps modernes.* Paris, 1960.

Bernot, Lucien, and René Blancard. *Nouville: Un village français.* Paris, 1953.

Bideau, A. "L'Envoi des jeunes enfants en nourrice. L'exemple d'une petite ville: Thoissey-en-Dombes (1740–1840)." In *Hommage à Marcel Reinhard: Sur la population française au XVIIIe et au XIXe siècles,* ed. Jacques Dupâquier. Paris, 1973.

Blayo, Yves. "La Mobilité dans un village de la Brie [Grisy-Suisnes, Seine-et-Marne] vers le milieu du XIXe siècle." *Population* 25, no. 3 (1970): 573–605.

——— and Louis Henry. "Données démographiques sur la Bretagne et l'Anjou de 1740 à 1789." *Annales de démographie historique,* 1967, pp. 91–171.

Bloch, Marc. "Les Transformations des techniques comme problèmes de psychologie collective." *Journal de psychologie normale et pathologique* 12 (1948): 104–120.

Blumin, Stuart. *The Urban Threshold: Growth and Change in a Nineteenth-Century American Community.* Chicago and London, 1976.

Bouchard, Gérard. *Le Village immobile: Sennely-en-Sologne au XVIIIe siècle.* Paris, 1972.

Bourgeois, Jean. "Le Mariage, coutume saisonnière: Contribution à l'étude sociologique de la nuptialité en France." *Population* 1, no. 4 (1946): 623–642.

Bourgeois-Pichat, J. "La Mesure de la mortalité infantile. I. Principes et méthodes. II. Les causes de décès." *Population* 6, nos. 2 and 3 (1951): 233–248 and 459–480.

———. "Evolution récente de la mortalité infantile." *Population* 19, no. 3 (1964): 417–438.

Bouvet, Michel. "Troarn: Etude de démographie historique (XVIIe– XVIIIe siècles)." In Michel Bouvet and Pierre Marie Bourdin, *A travers la Normandie des XVIIe et XVIIIe siècles*. Caen, 1968.

Burguière, André. *Bretons de Plozévet*. Paris, 1975.

Burnand, Robert. *La Vie quotidienne en France en 1830*. Paris, 1943.

Chamoux, Antoinette, and Cécile Dauphin. "La Contraception avant la Révolution française: L'exemple de Châtillon-sur-Seine." *Annales: Economies, Sociétés, Civilisations* 24, no. 3 (1969): 662–684.

Charbonneau, Hubert. *Tourouvre-au-Perche aux XVIIe et XVIIIe siècles: Etude de démographie historique*. Paris, 1970.

Chatelain, Abel. "La Migration viagère." *Annales: Economies, Sociétés, Civilisations* 2, no. 4 (1947): 411–416.

———. "Les Migrations temporaires françaises au XIXe siècle: Problèmes, méthodes, documentation." *Annales de démographie historique*, 1967, pp. 1–27.

———. "Migrations et domesticité féminine urbaine en France, XVIIIe–XXe siècles." *Revue d'histoire économique et sociale* 47 (1969): 506–528.

———. "Complexité des migrations temporaires et définitives à Paris et dans le bassin parisien, XVIIIe–XXe siècles." *Etudes de la région parisienne* 44 (1970): 1–10.

Chevalier, Louis, ed. *Le Choléra: La première épidémie du XIXe siècle*. La Roche-sur-Yon, 1958.

Choleau, Jean. *L'Expansion bretonne au XXe siècle*. Paris, 1922.

Couturier, Marcel. *Recherches sur les structures sociales de Châteaudun, 1525–1789*. Paris, 1969.

Cresset, J., and A. Troux. *La Géographie et l'histoire locales: Guide pour l'étude du milieu*. 4th ed. Paris, 1955.

Dansette, Adrien. *Histoire religieuse de la France contemporaine*. Rev. ed. Paris, 1965.

Delaunay, Paul. *La Maternité de Paris: Port-Royal de Paris.—Port-Libre.— L'Hospice de la Maternité.—L'Ecole des sages-femmes et ses origines (1625–1907)*. Paris, 1909.

Deniel, Raymond, and Louis Henry. "La Population d'un village du Nord de la France: Sainghin-en-Mélantois, de 1665 à 1851." *Population* 20, no. 4 (1965): 563–602.

Desaive, Jean-Paul, et al. *Médecins, climat, et épidémies à la fin du XVIIIe siècle*. Paris and The Hague, 1972.

Dunham, Arthur Louis. *The Industrial Revolution in France, 1815–1848*. New York, 1955.

Dupâquier, Jacques, and Marcel Lachiver. "Sur les débuts de la contraception en France ou les deux malthusianismes." *Annales: Economies, Sociétés, Civilisations* 24, no. 6 (1969): 1391–1406.

Dupin, Charles. *Forces productives et commerciales de la France*. 2 vols. Paris, 1827.

Duplessis–Le Guélinel, Gérard. *Les Mariages en France: Etude démographique.* Paris, 1954.

Duveau, Georges. *La Vie ouvrière en France sous le Second Empire.* Paris, 1946.

Duvignaud, Jean. *Change at Shebika: Report from a North African Village.* Trans. Frances Frenaye. New York, 1970.

Dyos, H. J. *Victorian Suburb: A Study of the Growth of Camberwell.* Leicester, 1961.

Flandrin, Jean-Louis. "Contraception, mariage et relations amoureuses dans l'occident chrétien." *Annales: Economies, Sociétés, Civilisations* 24, no. 6 (1969): 1370–1390.

————. *Les Amours paysannes: Amour et sexualité dans les campagnes de l'ancienne France (XVIe–XIXe siècles).* Paris, 1975.

Fleury, Michel, and Louis Henry. *Nouveau manuel de dépouillement et d'exploitation de l'état civil ancien.* Paris, 1965.

Ganiage, Jean. *Trois villages de l'Ile-de-France: Etude démographique.* Paris, 1963.

Ganiage, Jean A. "Aux confins de la Normandie: Structures de la natalité dans cinq villages du Beauvaisis." *Annales de Normandie* 23, no. 1 (1973): 57–90.

Gautier, Elie. *Un Siècle d'indigence: Pourquoi les Bretons s'en vont.* Paris, 1950.

Gautier, Etienne, and Louis Henry. *La Population de Crulai, paroisse normande: Etude historique.* Paris, 1958.

Gille, Bertrand. *Les Sources statistiques de l'histoire de France des enquêtes du 17e siècle à 1870.* Paris and Geneva, 1964.

Girard, Alain. *Démographie: Problèmes contemporains de population.* 2 vols. Paris, 1969.

Girard, Pierre. "Aperçus sur la démographie de Sotteville-lès-Rouen vers la fin du XVIIIe siècle." *Population* 14, no. 3 (1959): 485–508.

Gonnet, Paul. "Esquisse de la crise économique en France de 1827 à 1832." *Revue d'histoire économique et sociale* 33 (1955): 249–292.

Goubert, Jean-Pierre. *Malades et médecins en Bretagne, 1770–1790.* Paris, 1974.

Greven, Philip. *Four Generations: Population, Land, and Family in Colonial Andover, Massachusetts.* Ithaca and London, 1970.

Henry, Louis. *Manuel de démographie historique.* Rev. ed. Paris and Geneva, 1970.

———— and Claude Lévy. "Quelques données sur la région autour de Paris au XVIIIe siècle." *Population* 17, no. 2 (1962): 297–326.

Higonnet, Patrice L.-R. *Pont-de-Montvert: Social Structure and Politics in a French Village, 1700–1914.* Cambridge, Mass., 1971.

Hohenberg, Paul. "Change in Rural France in the Period of Industrialization, 1830–1914." *Journal of Economic History* 32 (1972): 219–240.

Houdaille, Jacques. "Monographie paroissiale sur la population

française au XVIIIe siècle: Un village du Morvan: Saint-Agnan."
Population 16, no. 2 (1961): 301–312.

———. "La Population de Boulay (Moselle) avant 1850." *Population* 22,
no. 2 (1967): 1055–1084.

Hunt, David. *Parents and Children in History: The Psychology of Family
Life in Early Modern France.* New York, 1970.

Isambert, François André. *Christianisme et classe ouvrière: Jalons pour une
étude de sociologie historique.* Paris, 1961.

Joanne, Adolphe. *Dictionnaire géographique de la France.* 2d ed. Paris,
1869.

Lachiver, Marcel. *La Population de Meulan du XVIIe au XIXe siècle (vers
1600–1870): Etude de démographie historique.* Paris, 1969.

Laslett, Peter. *The World We Have Lost.* New York, 1965.

Lees, Lynn H. "Patterns of Lower-Class Life: Irish Slum Communities
in Nineteenth-Century London." In *Nineteenth-Century Cities: Essays
in the New Urban History,* ed. Stephan Thernstrom and Richard Sennett. New Haven, 1969.

Lefranc, Georges. "The French Railroads, 1823–1842." *Journal of Economic and Business History* 2 (1930): 299–331.

Le Play, Frédéric. *Les Ouvriers européens.* 6 vols. Tours, 1878.

Le Roy Ladurie, Emmanuel. "Démographie et 'funestes secrets': Le
Languedoc (fin XVIIIe–début XIXe siècle)." *Annales historiques de la
révolution française* 37 (1965): 385–400.

Lhomme, Jean. "La Crise agricole à la fin du XIXe siècle en France:
Essai d'interprétation économique et sociale." *Revue économique* 21
(1970): 521–553.

McKeown, Thomas. *The Modern Rise of Population.* New York and San
Francisco, 1976.

Marcilhacy, Christiane. *Le Diocèse d'Orléans au milieu du XIXe siècle: Les
hommes et leurs mentalités.* Paris, 1964.

Mendras, Henri. *The Vanishing Peasant: Innovation and Change in French
Agriculture.* Trans. Jean Lerner. Cambridge, Mass., and London,
1970.

Mitchell, Donald W. "The French Railroad Attacks: February and
March 1848." Senior honors thesis, Harvard College, 1968.

Morin, Edgar. *Commune en France: La Métamorphose de Plodémet.* Paris,
1967.

Nadot, Robert. "Evolution de la mortalité infantile endogène en
France dans la deuxième moitié du XIXe siècle." *Population* 25, no. 1
(1970): 49–58.

Nettement, Alfred. *Mémoires historiques de S.A.R. Madame, Duchesse de
Berri depuis sa naissance jusqu'à ce jour.* 3 vols. Paris, 1837.

Newell, William H. "The Agricultural Revolution in Nineteenth-Century France." *Journal of Economic History* 33 (1973): 697–731.

Noilhan, Henri. *Histoire de l'agriculture à l'ère industrielle.* Paris, 1965.

Noonan, John T., Jr. *Contraception: A History of Its Treatment by the Catholic Theologians and Canonists.* Cambridge, Mass., 1965.

Pierrard, Pierre. *La Vie ouvrière à Lille sous le Second Empire.* Paris, 1965.

Pinchemel, Philippe. *Structures sociales et dépopulation rurale dans les campagnes picardes de 1836 à 1936.* Paris, 1957.

Pitié, Jean. *Exode rural et migrations intérieures en France: L'exemple de la Vienne et du Poitou-Charentes.* Poitiers, 1971.

Plaisse, André. *L'Evolution de la structure agraire dans la campagne de Neubourg.* Paris, 1964.

Ponteil, Félix. *Les Institutions de la France de 1814 à 1870.* Paris, 1966.

Powell, Sumner Clinton. *Puritan Village: The Formation of a New England Town.* Middletown, Conn., 1963.

Ranum, Orest, and Patricia Ranum, eds. *Popular Attitudes toward Birth Control in Pre-Industrial France and England.* New York, 1972.

Redfield, Robert. *Tepotzlán, a Mexican Village: A Study of Folk Life.* 2d ed. Chicago, 1947.

————. *A Village That Chose Progress: Chan Kom Revisited.* Chicago, 1950.

————. *The Little Community and Peasant Society and Culture.* Chicago, 1962.

———— and Alfonso Villa Rojas. *Chan Kom: A Maya Village.* 2d ed. Chicago, 1962.

Rigaudias-Weiss, Hilde. *Les Enquêtes ouvrières en France entre 1830 et 1848.* Paris, 1936.

Robiquet, Jean. *La Vie quotidienne au temps de Napoléon.* Paris, 1942.

Rosen, George. *A History of Public Health.* New York, 1958.

Rosenberg, Charles E. "Cholera in Nineteenth-Century Europe: A Tool for Social and Economic Analysis." *Comparative Studies in Society and History* 8 (1966): 452–463.

Rudé, George. *The Crowd in History: A Study of Popular Disturbances in France and England, 1730–1848.* New York, 1964.

Scott, Joan W. *The Glassworkers of Carmaux: French Craftsmen and Political Action in a Nineteenth-Century City.* Cambridge, Mass., 1974.

Sheppard, Thomas F. *Lourmarin in the Eighteenth Century: A Study of a French Village.* Baltimore and London, 1971.

Shorter, Edward. *The Historian and the Computer: A Practical Guide.* Englewood Cliffs, N.J., 1971.

————. *The Making of the Modern Family.* New York, 1975.

Sion, Jules. *Les Paysans de la Normandie orientale: Etude géographique sur les populations rurales du Caux et du Bray, du Vexin normand et de la vallée de la Seine.* Paris, 1908.

Sussman, George. "The Wet-nursing Business in Nineteenth-Century France." *French Historical Studies* 9, no. 2 (1975): 304–328.

Thabault, Roger. *1848–1914: L'Ascension d'un peuple: Mon village: Ses hommes, ses routes, son école.* Paris, 1944.

Thuillier, Guy. *Aspects de l'économie nivernaise au XIXe siècle.* Paris, 1966.

Vidalenc, Jean. "Les Résultats de l'enquête sur le travail prescrite par l'assemblée constituante dans le département de l'Eure." In *Actes du congrès historique du centenaire de la révolution de 1848.* Paris, 1948.

———. *Le Département de l'Eure sous la monarchie constitutionnelle, 1814– 1848.* Paris, 1952.

Warner, Charles K. "The 'Journal d'Agriculture Pratique' and the Peasant Question during the July Monarchy and the Second Republic." In *From the Ancien Régime to the Popular Front: Essays in the History of Modern France in Honor of Shepard B. Clough,* ed. Charles K. Warner. New York and London, 1969.

Weber, Eugen. *Peasants into Frenchmen: The Modernization of Rural France, 1870–1914.* Stanford, Calif., 1976.

Wylie, Laurence. "Demographic Change in Roussillon." In *Mediterranean Countrymen,* ed. Julian Pitt-Rivers. Paris and The Hague, 1963.

———. *Village in the Vaucluse.* Rev. ed. New York, 1964.

———, ed. *Chanzeaux: A Village in Anjou.* Cambridge, Mass., 1966.

Zeldin, Theodore. *France, 1848–1945.* Vol. 1: *Ambition, Love, and Politics.* London, 1970.

B. Works on the Seine-et-Oise and the greater Paris area

Barroux, Marius. *L'Ile-de-France et Saint-Denis.* Paris, 1938.

Bastié, Jean. *La Croissance de la banlieue parisienne.* Paris, 1964.

Bernard, Philippe. *Economie et sociologie de la Seine-et-Marne, 1850– 1950.* Paris, 1953.

Bruley, Edouard. *Seine-et-Oise.* Paris, 1928.

Cahen, Léon. "Ce qu'enseigne un péage au XVIIIe siècle: La Seine entre Rouen et Paris et les caractères de l'économie parisienne." *Annales d'histoire économique et sociale* 3 (1931): 487–518.

Chardonnet, M. "L'Industrie chimique dans la banlieue nord de Paris." *Bulletin de la société d'études historiques, géographiques, et scientifiques de la région parisienne* 21 (1947): 13–23.

Chatelain, Abel. "Brie: Terre de passage." *Annales: Economies, Sociétés, Civilisations* 4, no. 2 (1949): 159–166.

———. "Une Classe rurale au milieu du XIXe siècle: Les ouvriers agricoles de la Seine-et-Marne." *Bulletin de la société d'études historiques, géographiques, et scientifiques de la région parisienne* 27 (1953): 12–18.

———. "Evolution de la population de la banlieue parisienne (1876– 1962): L'inégal progrès de la proche banlieue: Seine-Banlieue." *Etudes de la région parisienne* 41 (1967): 43–46.

Chevalier, Louis. "Les Fondements économiques et sociaux de l'histoire politique de la région parisienne (1848–1370). Vol. 1: February 1848–December 1851." Thesis, University o Paris. Microfilm copy at Harvard University. [There is no vol. 2.]

Conac, Raoul. "Une Commune de la Seine de 1891 à 1911. Boulogne: évolution de la population et mouvement naturel." *Etudes de la région parisienne* 40 (July 1966): 9–13.

————. "Une Commune de la Seine de 1891 à 1911. Natalité et mortalité à Boulogne." *Etudes de la région parisienne* 40 (October 1966): 13–24.

Cornette, A. "La Dépopulation de Noyers-Saint-Martin (Oise) en un siècle, 1830–1930." *Bulletin de la société d'études historiques, géographiques, et scientifiques de la région parisienne* 6 (1932): 27–30.

Couard, Emile Louis. *L'Administration départementale de Seine-et-Oise, 1790–1913.* Versailles, 1913.

Couvreur, L., and E. Gautier. "Les Originaires de Bretagne dans l'agglomération parisienne, 1830–1949." *Bulletin de la société d'études historiques, géographiques, et scientifiques de la région parisienne* 26 (1952): 1–8.

Fourquin, Guy. *Les Campagnes de la région parisienne à la fin du moyen âge, du milieu du XIIIe au début du XVIe siècle.* Paris, 1964.

Hoss, Jean-Pierre. *Communes en banlieue: Argenteuil et Bezons.* Paris, 1969.

Joanne, Adolphe. *Géographie du département de Seine-et-Oise.* 5th ed. Paris, 1885.

Lachiver, Marcel. "Fécondité légitime et contraception dans la région parisienne." In *Hommage à Marcel Reinhard: Sur la population française au XVIIIe et au XIXe siècles,* ed. Jacques Dupâquier. Paris, 1973.

Lemoine, Henri. *Le Département de Seine-et-Oise de l'an VIII à 1871.* Paris, 1943.

Parrain, A. "Les Etrangers dans l'agriculture à Courdimanche (Seine-et-Oise)." *Bulletin de la société d'études historiques, géographiques, et scientifiques de la région parisienne* 12 (1938): 16–23.

Pédelaborde, Pierre. *L'Agriculture dans les plaines alluviales de la presqu'île de Saint-Germain-en-Laye: Le contact des structures rurale et urbaine.* Paris, 1961.

Phlipponeau, Michel. *La Vie rurale de la banlieue parisienne: Etude de géographie humaine.* Paris, 1956.

Rollet, Catherine, and Agnès Souriac. "Le Choléra de 1832 en Seine-et-Oise." *Annales: Economies, Sociétés, Civilisations* 29 (1974): 935–965.

Tricart, Jean. *La Culture fruitière dans la région parisienne.* Paris, 1948.

Tulippe, O. *L'Habitat rural en Seine-et-Oise: Essai de géographie de peuplement.* Liège, 1934.

Venard, Marc. *Bourgeois et paysans au XVIIe siècle: Recherche sur le rôle des bourgeois parisiens dans la vie agricole au sud de Paris au XVIIe siècle.* Paris, 1957.

C. Works on Bonnières and the Mantois

Anne, Albert. *La Houssaye et Noyon: Ancien domaine de Sully et de la duchesse de Berry.* Fécamp, 1963.

———. *Cent ans d'industrie bonnièroise, 1863–1963.* Mantes, 1964.

———. "Un Préfet bonnièrois: Armand Pihoret." *Le Mantois* 15 (1964): 24–30.

———. "La Légende des clés de ville à Freneuse." Reprinted separately from *Le Mantois* 20 (1969).

Béquin. "Quelques socialistes et anarchistes dans le Mantois de février 1848 à décembre 1851." *Le Mantois* 2 (1951): 5–8.

Bougeâtre, Eugène. *La Vie rurale dans le Mantois et le Vexin.* Meulan, 1971.

Cassan, Armand. *Statistique de l'arrondissement de Mantes.* Mantes, 1833.

Cobb, Richard C. "Les Disettes de l'an II et de l'an III dans le district de Mantes et la vallée de la basse Seine." *Mémoires de la Fédération des sociétés historiques et archéologiques de Paris et de l'Ile-de-France* 3 (1951): 227–251.

Deschamps, Georges. "Notes d'architecture rurale: Les fermes anciennes dans le Mantois." *Le Mantois* 4 (1953): 29–32.

Dupâquier, Jacques. "La Situation de l'agriculture dans le Vexin français (fin du XVIIIe siècle et début du XIXe siècle) d'après les enquêtes agricoles." In *Actes du 89e congrès national des sociétés savantes,* vol. 1. Lyons, 1964.

———. "Le Choléra de 1832 dans le Vexin français." *Mémoires de la société d'histoire et d'archéologie de l'arrondissement de Pontoise et du Vexin* 59 (1965): 72–82.

Dutois, (Abbé) François Napoléon. "Monographie de Bonnières: Notes manuscrites sur Bonnières et le canton." Ca. 1863. Albert Anne, Bonnières, has a typewritten transcription of this monograph.

Le Bomin, Philippe. "Les Evénements de 1848 à Mantes et leurs suites." *Le Mantois* 19 (1968): 3–27.

Poncelet, Maurice. *Histoire de la ville de Bonnières-sur-Seine.* Mantes, 1947.

Potié, M. "L'Opinion publique dans le Mantois au XIXe siècle." *Le Mantois* 12 (1961): 52–56.

Réaubourg, G. "L'Epidémie du choléra de 1832 dans le canton de Bonnières." *Bulletin de la société archéologique, historique, et scientifique de la région de Bonnières* 1924, no. 8: 143–145.

Subtil, G. "Histoire des chemins de fer dans la région mantaise." *Le Mantois* 10 (1959): 1–4.

———. "Un Voyage de Paris à Rouen en 1843." *Le Mantois* 11 (1960): 10–13.

Tercinet, M. "Le Jeu de tamis dans le Mantois." *Le Mantois* 4 (1953): 16–17.

Walter, Rodolphe, "Emile Zola et Paul Cézanne à Bennecourt en 1866." *Le Mantois* 12 (1961): 1–40.

———. "Un Vrai Cézanne: 'La vue de Bonnières.' " *Gazette des Beaux-Arts* 61 (1963): 359–366.

Index

Library of Congress Cataloging in Publication Data

Ackerman, Evelyn Bernette.
  Village on the Seine.

  Bibliography: p.
  Includes index.
  1. Bonnières-sur-Seine, France—History. 2. Bonnières-sur-Seine,
France—Social conditions. 3. Bonnières-sur-Seine, France—Economic
conditions.
  I. Title.
DC801.B693A34   944'.36   78-58071
  ISBN 0-8014-1178-5

087662